DATE DUE

WOMEN IN SOCIETY

BRAZIL

JANE KOHEN WINTER

MARSHALL CAVENDISH
New York • London • Sydney

Reference edition published 1993 by
Marshall Cavendish Corporation
2415 Jerusalem Avenue
P.O. Box 587
North Bellmore
New York 11710

© Times Editions Pte Ltd 1993

Originated and designed by
Times Books International, an imprint of
Times Editions Pte Ltd

Printed in Singapore

Library of Congress Cataloging-in-Publication Data:
Winter, Jane Kohen,
     Women in society. Brazil/ Jane Kohen Winter
       p. cm.—(Women In Society)
     Includes bibliographical references and index.
     Summary: Provides a historical overview of the experiences
of women in Brazilian society, discussing their participation
in various fields and profiling the lives of significant women.
     ISBN 1-85435-558-9
     1. Women—Brazil—Social conditions—Juvenile literature
[1. Women—Brazil.] 2. Brazil—Social conditions.] I. Title.
II. Series: Women in society (New York, N.Y.)
HQ1542.W56 1993
305.42'0981—dc20   92–34403
                                        CIP
                                          AC

51970

Women in Society
Editorial Director   Shirley Hew
Managing Editor   Shova Loh
Editors   Irene Toh
                                          Vijaya Radhakrishnan
                                          Goh Sui Noi
                                          Sue Sismondo
                                          Maureen Kelly
                                          Andrea Borch
                                          MaryLee Knowlton
Picture Editor   Yee May Kaung
Production   Edmund Lam
Design   Tuck Loong
                                          Ronn Yeo
                                          Felicia Wong
                                          Loo Chuan Ming
Illustrators   Jimmy Kang
                                          Kelvin Sim
MCC Editorial Director   Evelyn M. Fazio

94-18873

Introduction

Brazil is one of the world's largest, most populous, and most fascinating countries. Colonized in the early part of the 16th century by the Portuguese, Brazil has a strong patriarchal tradition common to Iberian cultures. For centuries, the gender roles of Brazilians were sharply defined—women were the rulers of the household while men had power in the world outside the home. In just the last few decades, however, a significant shift in society has taken place. The country has become primarily urban, and women have had to leave home for the workplace. Still, although women have made important inroads into the professions, Brazilian society continues to be dominated by men.

It is impossible to generalize about the "woman's experience" in Brazil without considering economic standing, social class, and color. We will examine what life is like for Brazilian women from various regions with different religious, family, and ethnic backgrounds. Chapter 1 starts with the tale of a powerful African-Brazilian goddess who, even today, is an influence in women's lives. Chapter 2 gives an overview of Brazilian women from the earliest times to the present. The achievements of women in different areas of society are dealt with in Chapter 3. Chapter 4 discusses Brazilian religions and ethnic groups. Chapter 5 gives detailed profiles of some of Brazil's most exceptional women, and finally, Chapter 6 describes the important rituals and rites of passage of the Brazilian woman from childhood to old age.

Contents

chapter one

Yemanjá

Before the sun rises on February 2nd in the coastal city of Salvador de Bahia, groups of Brazilians meet in the quiet square of a 100-year-old Catholic Church. They have gathered to honor the patron saint of Bahia, the powerful Yemanjá, goddess of the sea, who is closely identified with the Virgin Mary.

First, the worshipers offer Yemanjá her favorite food, a mixture of corn, palm oil, and onion. Then a group of drummers gathers under a small hut with a roof of palm leaves and beats out an entrancing rhythm to lure the goddess to the site. When the bright, clear Bahian sun rises, more followers of Yemanjá begin to gather in large groups near the shore close to the church. Slowly, the beach fills up with thousands and thousands of worshipers—mostly women and children.

Brazilian women of all social classes and skin colors come to the seashore to offer the goddess a special gift in exchange for a personal favor. Some women ask the goddess to help them find a husband or a good job. Some ask her to keep their children healthy or for general good luck. Fishermen's wives ask her to keep their husbands' nets full. Childless women ask to be blessed with fertility. Many of these women would probably call themselves Catholic if asked about their religion, but on this day they pay homage to the African aspect of their country, the part that has brought Brazil its spicy food, its exciting samba music and dance, its folk culture, its color, its imagination, and its spirituality.

Opposite: A celebrant asking for the blessings of Yemanjá on New Year's Eve in Rio de Janeiro.

Right: Statue of Yemanjá

Ritual offering

The women place their gifts in large wicker baskets that will later be taken out to sea by Bahian fishermen. At the appointed hour, the fishermen load the weighty wicker baskets onto boats and sail out to sea. All at once, the precious gifts are thrown into the waves.

If they sink, it means that the goddess is pleased with her presents and will grant the wishes of the givers. If they float, the worshipers will have to wait another year for their needs to be met.

Different worship rituals

Yemanjá is worshiped in other Brazilian cities in different ways.

In Rio de Janeiro, her celebrants dress completely in white and gather by the tens of thousands on the shores of the city's magnificent beaches on New Year's Eve. At the stroke of midnight, some wade into the surf and throw white flowers to the goddess. Others light candles and perch them atop miniature boats that they push into the sea at the appointed time.

On the island of Itaparica, Yemanjá

is worshiped by the high priestesses of *candomblé* ("cahn-dom-BLEH"), an African-Brazilian religion. These priestesses, dressed in elegant, lacy white dresses, carry wicker baskets on their heads and travel with the fishermen and some drummers and singers on the boats. When the music reaches a fever pitch, the priestesses throw their parcels overboard and then enter a trance of spirit possession.

A feminine image

Yemanjá has strictly feminine tastes, so her followers often give her flowers, perfumes, fans, mirrors, hair ribbons, dolls, face powders, and sweet-smelling soaps. Yemanjá's favorite colors are white and blue, the colors of the sea, so many of the gifts come in these colors. Statues of the goddess depict her as a voluptuous woman with jet black hair and eyes, and stark white skin. She often wears a glittering crown and a long blue or white dress. The fact that the goddess is so feminine is interesting because Brazilian women are said to be extremely feminine.

The influence of the Sea Goddess

The worship of Yemanjá, in all its manifestations, and of other African-Brazilian gods and goddesses, is an important part of Brazilian culture. Yemanjá gives women optimism for the future and acts as an outlet for their hopes and dreams. To many she is a mother figure, life-giving and generous. To others she is a protector against evil and misfortune.

To many black Brazilians, Yemanjá is also a symbol of resistance to the former repression of black African slaves who were forced to sail to Brazil during the colonial days to work in the country's vast plantations. Because the slaves were coerced into converting to Catholicism, many pretended to honor the Virgin Mary and Jesus Christ in their new home, while they were actually praying to their own African gods, including Yemanjá and her husband, Oxalá, the creator god.

Today when black Brazilians pay homage to Yemanjá, they are remembering the suffering of their enslaved ancestors and asserting their cultural identity as blacks in a country where slavery existed until the late 19th century. In recent years, Yemanjá has become quite popular among people of all races in Brazil.

A priestess during prayer on Rio de Janeiro's Copacabana Beach.

Yemanjá is proof of the tolerance of Brazilians for other religions and of the widespread belief in the magical world of the spirits that so pervades Brazilian society.

chapter two

Milestones

T he history of Brazilian women, from pre-colonial days to the present, is a fascinating one. Although women as a whole certainly did not have an active voice during much of Brazil's history, they played more important roles than many historical accounts would lead one to believe.

Before the arrival of the Portuguese colonists in the early 16th century, Brazil was inhabited by various Indian tribes with different languages and customs. In many tribes, women served a vital purpose within the community as they shared much of the work with the men and helped the tribe survive. When the Portuguese colonized Brazil, intermarriage between European men and Indian women took place. The intermingling of cultures expanded in the 17th and 18th centuries with the arrival of black slaves from Africa.

In the 19th century, Brazil's cities began to grow. Women, especially those of the lower classes, started to work, first in home industries and later, outside the home. The women's suffrage movement in Brazil began in the first decades of the 20th century. By 1932, women were given the right to vote, but their lives changed little until quite recently.

Pre-colonial history

Before the Portuguese found their way to Brazil in 1500, the country was populated by 3 to 5 million Indians of hundreds of different tribes.

Opposite and *right:* Brazilian women today enjoy far greater freedom and opportunities for work than those who lived even two or three decades ago. The picture on the right shows an artist.

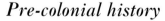

The Indians of Brazil were not as developed as their Aztec and Inca counterparts to the north and west. Their customs varied from tribe to tribe. For the most part, tribes lived a semi-nomadic existence

Every few years, the tribe found a new site near a water source and built a large communal hut. The women planted crops while the men hunted for small animals. Once the food supply was exhausted, the tribe burned the fields to fertilize them for future use and moved on to a new site.

The tribes that historians know the most about were those on the north-eastern coast of Brazil where the colonists first settled. These tribes, for the most part, spoke the Tupi language. Within the tribe, men and women had very distinct tasks assigned to them, with women doing the bulk of the work. The men were responsible for burning the forests, looking for firewood, hunting, fishing, and guarding the tribe against attackers and wild animals. Experts with bows and arrows, they were fierce warriors who were said to cannibalize the enemies they captured.

The Indian tribeswomen The women's tasks were more labor intensive than the men's. The average tribeswoman was responsible for planting crops and gathering water. She was also in charge of weaving cotton hammocks that served as beds for the entire tribe. She made cups, bowls, and jugs out of clay—these were fired in a hole dug into the ground.

The most important task of the tribal woman was preparing food. Although many tribes planted small fields of yams, gourds, corn, and peanuts, the primary food source was manioc or cassava, that the women, through a long process, turned into flour. They performed this elaborate process with small children slung across their backs or carried on their hips. Manioc was also mixed with water for various drinks and fermented into a kind of wine. Women kept the hut orderly and, in some tribes, domesticated the animals. The Indian woman was so accustomed to intensive labor, in fact, that when the colonists appeared, she was better prepared to work for them than was her husband.

Colonial Brazil

The first Portuguese man to reach the

Turning manioc into food

First, the manioc root was dug up from the earth and soaked in water for a period of days, to remove the tough outer rind and soften the meat. Then the manioc was mashed by hand, strained to rid it of excess moisture, and placed in the sun to dry. Finally, it was dried in an oven, and then baked with other ingredients into breads, cakes, puddings, and pastries.

coast of Brazil was Pedro Alvares Cabral, who arrived in what is now called Porto Seguro in April, 1500. Cabral was supposedly in search of India, but went off course and happened upon Brazil, one of the largest land masses in the world. The Indians were friendly to Cabral, but he stayed only a matter of days before deciding to return to Portugal with samples of a hard wood called brazilwood, from which the country later got its name.

In 1532, the first permanent Portuguese settlement was founded in Brazil, near São Paulo. In 1549, the first official governor was sent from Portugal to Bahia in the northeast of Brazil to establish the seat of government. One thousand settlers accompanied the governor. Together they founded what was and still is the only Portuguese-speaking nation in all of Latin America.

Intermarriage with Amerindian women There were few white women among the initial groups of Portuguese settlers. The white Portuguese men were eager to marry the native Amerindian women and populate the vast land they had claimed for the Portuguese crown. In Brazil, the transfer of power from the natives to the colonists appeared to be more harmonious and less violent, at least initially, than in other South American countries colonized by the Spanish.

The female natives, for the most part, willingly married the Portuguese men and were baptized into the Catholic tradition. The tribeswoman brought her knowledge of plants and animals and her culinary traditions to her marriage, serving as an asset to the inexperienced Portuguese settler trying to survive in an unfamiliar land.

Sugar plantations The early settlers soon found out that the soil of the northeast was well-suited to the planting of sugarcane. By 1600, Brazil had 200 sugar mills.

A black slave working on a sugar plantation. When the Portuguese could not enslave enough Brazilian Indians to work on their sugar plantations, they brought in Afican slaves, both men and women, as workers.

Plantation life: the big house

The stable element in Portuguese-Brazilian (or "Luso-Brazilian," as it is called) society throughout the colonial era, which continued into the 19th century, was the plantation. The typical plantation was a large, self-sufficient agricultural concern. It consisted of many acres of fields, a mansion where the white man and his family lived called the big house, and slave quarters that usually housed from 100 to 150 black slaves. During the early years of colonialism, Brazil's primary crop was sugar, which was cultivated in the north. Later, coffee, grown in the south, became the country's largest export crop.

Many of the big houses in colonial Brazil were wide, spacious two-story structures with large kitchens and dining rooms, many bedrooms, parlors for entertaining guests, small rooms for house slaves, wings for grown sons and their families, and rooms in the center of the house for unmarried daughters. The mansions were often surrounded by well-planted gardens decorated with ponds, aviaries with exotic birds, and dove cotes. The property contained a well, chicken coops, pig pens, a stable and, perhaps a short distance away, the *senzala* ("say-ZELL-ah") or slave quarters. Often the big house and its grounds were surrounded by a wall.

The Portuguese planted on a large scale. Each plantation required more than 100 laborers to tend the fields and process the cane. Initially, the settlers attempted to force the native Brazilians into slavery. Groups of raiders made expeditions into Brazil's vast interior to round up Indians and sell them into slavery in São Paulo. The expeditions were called *bandeiras*, which means "flags," and the men who took part were called *bandeirantes* ("bahn-day-RANT-ees").

The Indians, previously eager to trade goods with the settlers, did not go into bondage willingly. Some died in battles with the Portuguese. Others, after being captured, died while working on the plantations. Most, however, caught the deadly diseases brought by the Portuguese from Europe—smallpox, tuberculosis, typhus, scurvy, and the most destructive, syphilis—and died because their bodies had no resistance to the foreign illnesses. With little hope of enslaving the native Brazilians on a scale big enough to meet the needs of the large, prosperous sugar plantations, the Portuguese turned to Africa for their slaves.

African slavery In the middle of the 16th century, the first black African slaves—both men and women—were brought to Brazil by European sea captains who traded them for tobacco and liquor. Many slaves came from the western and central parts of Africa—Nigeria, the Congo, and the Ivory Coast—and were sent to work the fields in Bahia and Pernambuco. Some went to Rio de Janeiro, which was founded in 1567. The journey by ship was extremely brutal, and many of the slaves died before they reached Brazil. By 1600, approximately 30,000 Portuguese settlers, 20,000 black slaves, and thousands of Indian slaves lived and worked in Portuguese settlements. As many as 1,500 slaves arrived every year.

The Luso-Brazilian woman

The white Luso-Brazilian woman lived a relatively secluded life within the walls of her large plantation house. Her husband was the patriarch or head of the family, and his word was absolute.

According to an old Portuguese saying, a proper white woman of the upper classes was to leave her home only three times during her life—"to be baptized, to be married, and to be buried." Most Luso-Brazilian women went to church every Sunday, but always in the company of other family members. An estate often had its own chapel, and the women had no need to leave her property to worship.

> The big house occupied an important place in Luso-Brazilian society.

The life of the white Luso-Brazilian woman of the colonial era was one of seclusion.

Literacy During much of the colonial era, few women knew how to read, so they were unable to spend their time studying or reading the Bible. In fact, women were considered unworthy of any kind of education at all. Some men believed that women were biologically incapable of learning or that their brains were too small to hold knowledge!

Mistress of the household Many upper-class women had little to do within the home as the cleaning chores, cooking, and heavy work were done by black house slaves. Some of them took control of domestic activities by directing the servants. The mistress provided supervision in these areas: spinning, weaving, sewing, lacemaking, embroidery, the preparation of meals, the maintenance of the orchards and garden, and the care of the children. She was also the organizer of big social events hosted by her family.

Although strong, mature women could certainly find satisfaction within the home, many women were simply too immature to manage their own households. Girls were often married at the age of 13 to men who were considerably older and more worldly. Many girls simply went from the cloistered world of childhood, in which their every move was scrutinized by fathers and brothers, into the equally constraining world of marriage, in which their husbands kept watch over them.

Some women left their homes to pay social calls on other women, but they traditionally wore veils to cover their faces and heavy garments to hide their arms and legs, even in hot weather.

The ladies typically wore a good deal of gold jewelry and were carried about in their hammocks or palanquins, box-like enclosures mounted on poles and lifted by four slaves.

Marriage Both fathers and older brothers considered it their duty to protect the reputations of the women of the household, for virtue, purity, and virginity were of utmost importance for girls if they wished to marry. One of the most significant decisions for a father was the selection of a husband for his daughter. It was not uncommon for the girl to have little firsthand knowledge of her husband until just before the marriage ceremony.

If the bride-to-be was dissatisfied with her father's choice, she felt it her duty to obey him anyway. Marriage arrangements were made on a monetary rather than romantic basis. Girls were expected to have demure, compliant personalities, and those who were outspoken or disobedient were reprimanded by mothers and fathers alike.

Childbirth and its effects After marriage, women were expected to start having children immediately. They were encouraged to have as many as possible in an effort to populate the country and leave the family financially secure should the head of the family die suddenly.

It is no wonder, then, that foreigners who passed through Brazil and returned home to publish accounts of their experiences described the colonial woman as a listless creature looking older than her years due to the strain of

"Marriages are formed when the parties are very young, and it is by no means uncommon to meet with mothers not 13 years old. The climate and the retired habits of the Brazilian woman have, early in life, a considerable effect on their appearance. When extremely young, the fine dark eyes and full person make them generally admired, but a few years work a change in their appearance ..."
—*Alexander Caldcleugh*
Travels in South America in the Years 1819, 1820, 1821

countless childbirths and spending her days dressed in a loosely fitting garment to keep her cool in the hot climate, swinging in a hammock, taking naps, and gossiping with her servants.

A girl's choices: marriage or the convent

For white Luso-Brazilian girls from respected families, colonial society offered only two choices: marriage to a man handpicked by the girl's parents or life in a Catholic convent.

Marriage dowry Marriage was preferred, because it gave the girl's family the opportunity to expand its financial holdings and form a bond with other members of the elite class. In the early years of colonialism, much of a family's property was passed from generation to generation in the form of a marriage dowry given to the daughter.

The following list of goods is a sample of a real dowry that was registered in São Paulo in May of 1641. It is interesting to note that the parents of Maria de Proença, the bride, put their daughter on the list, along with the slaves, and what we might consider trivial possessions such as dishes and pots. Items from the dowry include:

- their daughter dressed in black satin, with two other fine dresses, gold earrings, and a gold necklace
- a bed with its curtains and linens
- a table and six chairs
- a buffet, tablecloths, and towels
- thirty china dishes
- two chests with locks
- a large and a small copper pot
- a tiled house and a farm in São Sebastião
- a field of manioc and a field of cotton
- a house in town
- twenty agricultural tools
- two African and 30 Indian slaves
- one boat or canoe with oars
- five hundred bags of flour

In the 17th century, these gifts were often so extravagant that little was left to bequeath to the sons. Many men, therefore, had little way of gaining riches other than to marry well. After the marriage, the wife's dowry and the husband's money legally belonged to both parties.

A dowry was amassed from the moment of a girl's birth, when she received presents from relatives. Through the dowry, parents were able to choose a suitable son-in-law. In this way, they retained control over their daughter's future life and prevented their own property from being badly managed by a son-in-law of whom they did not approve.

In the 18th century, dowries became less extravagant and sons were able to inherit more property upon their parents' death. As society changed and men were able to make their own fortunes, through business for instance, girls lost their edge in the marriage market. Wealthy sons-in-law became favored over wealthy daughters-in-law.

Entering the convent If a white girl of the upper class did not marry, either because her family could not afford to give her a dowry or because a suitable match could not be made, she might choose to stay at home and see her parents into old age. But more often she entered a convent, where she lived for the rest of her life. Some parents placed very young daughters in convents until they were old enough to be married.

The convent offered parents the assurance that their daughter's virtue would be protected and the family's reputation would remain unblemished. Some girls joined convents in Brazil, while others were sent to Portugal. Parents often had a difficult time finding a convent for their daughters because so many other parents were competing for the same places.

The girl's family had to pay dearly for her place in the convent. There was an annual fee for upkeep, and an additional sum when the girl took her vows. The nuns of the convent often taught their young charges how to read and write—something girls were denied in the outside world—and gave lessons in music and art.

The black slave woman

The black slave woman of Brazil led an extremely difficult life. She had no legal rights. She led a life of relentless subservience, whether in the fields or in the kitchen of the big house.

The lowest in society Many black slaves came from African civilizations that were more developed—agriculturally, politically, and artistically—than that of the Portuguese in Brazil. They were torn from a society in which they were full and equal members into one in which they formed the lowest rung on the societal ladder.

Her work and lifestyle Female slaves worked both in the fields and the big house. Many slaves were not strong enough for field work, so they were given other tasks. Women often worked as cooks, waitresses or maids to the ladies of the big house. Older slave women looked after both black and white

children. Because they breastfed, dressed, bathed, and played with the children, they often developed a strong sense of attachment to their charges. At night, they told the children fairy tales based on African myths and sang them to sleep.

Other female slaves were responsible for washing clothes—a very difficult and time-consuming process in those times.

A house slave being supervised closely by her mistress.

A day on a coffee plantation

Life on a coffee plantation is a subject that has fascinated writers and historians of Brazilian society. One of them, Stanley Stein—who has done extensive work on the subject—reconstructed a typical day on a Brazilian coffee plantation in the 19th century.

Work often started before dawn. Awakened by the repeated gong of a large bell, the slaves rose from the wooden beds in their tiny rooms, washed quickly and met the master of the house on the terrace for the morning prayer and the day's work orders. After a small breakfast of corn bread and coffee, some slaves went to the big house to receive work instructions from the mistress. Most, however, picked up their tools and walked to the area of the plantation they had been assigned to weed that day. Elderly slave women were often given the rows nearest to their living quarters. New mothers brought along their infants on their backs. Children under 10 kept close to their mothers on the way to the fields and were allowed to play nearby. Teenaged children were expected to work alongside adults.

The work became considerably more difficult as the heat rose, and as the slaves, both female and male, progressed further up the hills with their hoes. To help pass the time and to create a rhythmic pace, they sang African and Portuguese songs together. They would occasionally pause for a brief moment to smoke a pipe. The bell for lunch would ring at about 10 a.m. The slaves would walk down the hill for a quick break, during which the mothers would have a chance to feed their babies. Field work would be interrupted again at 1 p.m. for coffee, and at 4 p.m. for supper, after which the slaves would work until the sun went down. Some slaves were given night chores, such as hulling rice, preparing manioc flour and making cornmeal. It would take them until 10 or 11 p.m. to complete these chores.

In some households, the mistress and the slaves had an amiable relationship. In others, the relationship was strained because the mistress found fault with the slaves' work. The house slave or *mucama* ("moo-CAH-ma") often had less intensive work to do than those working in the fields, but her freedom was even more curtailed because her mistress kept a close watch at all times.

The last chore of the day for the *mucama* was to clean the feet of her mistress. Sometimes, house slaves were locked in their rooms during the night. For many slaves, their only freedom came on Saturday evening, when they were allowed to congregate for dancing and singing, and Sunday afternoon, when they were given leave to tend to the small gardens given to them by their masters and take care of their own household chores.

Sexual intermingling

Throughout the colonial era, Brazil was known for its relaxed attitude toward relationships among people of different races. The Catholic Church was even said to approve of sex outside marriage if it led to children who would populate the colony.

It was quite common, in fact, for the white male of the manor to take a black African slave (and/or a native Amerindian woman) as his mistress and to produce mulatto children with her. During the early centuries of colonialism, the children of these unions were born into slavery. However, in many families, the racially mixed children of the master and the slave woman were brought into the big house and given the same opportunities as their white half brothers and sisters.

In many situations, the white man's Portuguese wife would have full knowledge of her husband's activities but was unable to do anything about them. This situation was often a source of great frustration for the white woman, who would take out her jealous feelings in the form of verbal or even physical abuse on the black mistress. In Luso-Brazilian society, promiscuity by men was condoned, even applauded by society; for a woman, especially a white Catholic woman, promiscuity was the greatest of sins.

During the 18th century in the Brazilian region of Minas Gerais, it was the habit of white males to take light-skinned black women as concubines and to make them maids, cooks or house-keepers within the big house. These women, called *minas*, were said to be quite respected by their white masters. They were consulted on important household decisions, admired for their efficiency and cherished for their companionship. Some white men even married their *minas*, thereby making their children legitimate and legally able to inherit property.

Sexual intermingling in Brazil produced a people of mixed heritage.

Nearly 30% of the homes in São Paulo in 1765 were headed by women. By 1802, the figure had risen to an amazing 45%. By 1836, there were more female-headed households than male-headed ones in São Paulo.

The female head of household

During the colonial era, it was common for a white woman to be suddenly thrust into the position of being the head of the household. Because girls were married so young to men who were one or two generations older, women often became widows at an early age.

In other instances, the male head of the household would go into the interior of the country on an Indian slaving expedition or in search of gold in Minas Gerais or Mato Grosso, never to return. Other women were simply deserted by their husbands.

A position of responsibility What were the concerns and responsibilities of a female head of household? She had many burdens to shoulder. She was forced to take an authoritative position in a patriarchal society where men were the absolute leaders.

Within the home, the widow became solely responsible for raising and protecting her small children. Her daughters had to be taught the proper domestic skills to mold them into good wives. Her sons had to be educated in mathematics, reading, and writing. They had to be taught either a trade or how to manage the family estate. All the children had to be given adequate religious instruction. In addition, she had to take charge of the family farm (at least until she married again, as widows often did).

Official records indicate that in the 17th century there were many female sugarcane growers. In the 18th century there were women cattle ranchers, small farmers, shopkeepers, and gold mine operators. To the white woman in the colonial era, widowhood often brought her into greater contact with people outside the home and the church, thus enabling her to expand her world.

The white woman who did not wish to assume responsibility for her household after her husband's death often left affairs in the hands of a brother or an eldest son and took up residence in a respectable retirement home.

The breadwinner role Female heads of households were quite common in Brazil's urban areas, especially among women of the lower classes, who were not required to isolate themselves as much as their white, upper-class counterparts.

Many of them were members of the

lower class. They supported themselves and their families by starting small businesses such as textile workshops within the home. Cotton was purchased in bulk at a large market, then brought home to be spun, dyed and woven by mothers, aunts, and daughters.

Some women ran small shops that sold fruits, vegetables, poultry, and other food, as well as general items. Some women sold cooked food or sweets on the streets or peddled their dishes from house to house. Others took in laundry or ran boarding houses, taverns, or slaughterhouses. Some women worked as hairdressers or midwives. Many women who had no other means of supporting themselves turned to prostitution.

Brazil in the 19th century

The 19th century was an era of tremendous change for Brazil, as it was for many other Latin American countries.

In 1807, just a few days before Napoleon Bonaparte of France invaded Lisbon, Portugal, the Portuguese monarchy set off for Brazil. Upon the arrival of the queen and her son, the crown prince Dom João (and their 15,000 attendants), Brazil became the first and only colonial outpost to house a European royal family.

Dom João decreed a number of reforms, one of which was the practical recognition of Brazil as the seat of government for its mother county, Portugal.

In 1822, under the leadership of Dom João's son, Dom Pedro, Brazil severed its ties with Portugal and became independent.

One way female breadwinners in the 19th century made a living was to sell wares on the street.

The growth of cities Although in the first centuries of colonialism Brazil was a land of extremes in terms of class structure—there were the "haves" and the "have-nots"—this began to change in the 19th century.

The Brazilian economy was still primarily agricultural, but the cities were beginning to become commercial centers. Rio had 60,000 inhabitants in 1808, and more than 120,000 just 15 years later. Following Rio, Salvador and Recife were the second and third most populous cities after the first quarter of the 19th century.

In the 19th century, members of the upper class spent time both on their rural estates and in their smaller urban mansions.

Life in the city Being in the city was an eye-opening experience for the upper-class Brazilian woman who had until then led a life of near seclusion in the country.

The city offered women a host of amusements. Women led a more sociable lifestyle. They could go to the theater, have coffee at a café with friends, go to parties or shop. They dressed more fashionably. With the arrival of the Portuguese royal family in Rio de Janeiro in 1808, upper-class women were introduced to the newest

European fashions and began to imitate them.

For the lower-class women, the city offered a life of few restrictions. These women could work and travel about unchaperoned. Slaves living in the cities were often allowed to meet friends at night. Some were allowed by their masters to start small street vending businesses.

Although women of all social classes were given greater freedom in the cities, they were still excluded from positions of power in government, politics, commerce, and the home.

Empress Leopoldina

One of the more exceptional women of 19th century Brazil was Leopoldina. She was an Austrian-born archduchess who became empress of Brazil upon her marriage.

Girlhood In 1797, Leopoldina was born into the powerful Hapsburg family of Austria. Her father was Franz I, and her sister, Marie Louise, had an ill-fated marriage to Napoleon Bonaparte of France.

Leopoldina was an attractive but by no means beautiful girl. She had no use for the superficialities of court life, and was more inclined toward studying and listening to music than dressing up in ornate royal costumes and participating in court intrigues. Her passions were books and horseback riding. She was

well-versed in the natural sciences, history and foreign languages.

Marriage In 1816, a marriage was arranged between Leopoldina and Pedro of the house of Braganza, the family that had ruled Portugal and Brazil for nearly two centuries.

The dowry was fixed at 200,000 florins (a type of gold coin used in Europe at the time) with an additional annual payment of 80,000 florins.

Empress Leopoldina. She was admired by the Brazilian people for her intelligence and commitment to the independence movement.

In May of 1817, at the age of 20, Leopoldina was married in a lavish ceremony in Vienna to a representative of the Portuguese crown. The groom did not attend the ceremony but waited for his bride in Brazil.

When Leopoldina met her husband several months later in Rio de Janeiro after a lengthy sea voyage, she was impressed by his handsome features and manly grace and became immediately devoted to him.

Later, after another marriage ceremony, she found that they had much in common: he was an excellent horseman and was very fond of music. This pleased her very much.

Leopoldina, now a princess, found much to admire about her new home too. She loved Brazil's magnificent landscapes and took an immediate interest in its people, although they were quite different from her fellow Austrians. The Brazilian people soon came to revere her as well.

Birth In 1819, the princess gave birth to her first child, a daughter named Maria da Glória. In the years that followed, she had several miscarriages that left her depressed and anxious for a son who could inherit the throne. In March of 1821, a son, Dom João Carlos, was finally born, although he died before reaching his first birthday. Another daughter, named Januaria, followed soon after.

Coming to the throne Later that year, the king and queen gathered the gold of Brazil's treasury and boarded a ship for Portugal, never to return, leaving Leopoldina and Pedro in full charge of the country.

The months that followed were tense, as the native Brazilians battled for independence from Portugal, a move that was wholeheartedly supported by the princess. Under her influence, Pedro came to believe fiercely in Brazil's independence. Soon after 1822, Dom Pedro was crowned emperor of Brazil and Leopoldina became his empress.

A love betrayed In 1822, Dom Pedro fell in love with another woman, Domitila de Castro, who was said to be far more beautiful—and cunning—than

> "For almost four years...for love of a seductive monster I have been reduced to the state of greatest slavery and totally forgotten by my adored Pedro. Lately I have received final proof that he has forgotten me in the presence of that very one who is the cause of all my afflictions....Ah! My beloved daughters! What will become of you after my death!?..."
> —*Empress Leopoldina,
> in a letter to her sister*

Empress Leopoldina. This affair, which Dom Pedro took no pains to hide, became a source of outrage for Brazilians both within and outside the court.

To Leopoldina, it became the bane of her existence. The intimacy that she had shared with her husband was shattered, and she felt very much alone in the court. Nevertheless, she felt it her duty to hide her humiliation and distress for fear it would harm Brazil's reputation in Europe.

Dom Pedro II In 1824, both Domitila and Leopoldina gave birth to sons by Dom Pedro. Domitila's son died soon after birth, but Leopoldina's son, Dom Pedro II, later became a benevolent, much respected leader who ruled Brazil for 50 years. His accomplishments include the refinement of the parliamentary system and the abolition of slavery.

The long-suffering wife In 1825, Dom Pedro gave Domitila a noble title and insisted that she lived at the court, a move that horrified Leopoldina's father, the Emperor of Austria. In 1826, in a final affront, Dom Pedro bestowed noble titles on the members of Domitila's family. Within a few months, Leopoldina had a miscarriage and was stricken with a deadly fever that left her delirious and under the delusion that her husband's mistress was trying to harm her son. She died a sad woman.

Women and education

During most of the 19th century, education was an exclusive privilege of upper-class men. An overwhelming majority of women were without reading or writing skills of any kind.

Today, girls and boys alike go to school. Until the last part of the 19th century, girls were taught only domestic skills.

"A girl who knows a lot is a mixed-up girl. To be a good mother, one should know little or nothing."
—*Old Brazilian adage*

A school in a village in the Amazon region. Although teaching was (and still is) a low-paying profession in Brazil, it is considered a decent, honest occupation for a girl.

Because women were confined to the domestic world, it was thought that they need not learn to read anything beyond recipes and the Bible. Men even feared the idea of education for women because, as one Brazilian wrote in 1834, "if a woman knew how to read, she would be able to receive love letters."

Even as late as 1872, only about 1 million free men, 550,000 free women, 900 slave men, and 440 slave women could read, out of a national population of more than 10 million.

In the mid-19th century, some upper-class girls attended schools where they learned domestic and social skills, including cooking, needlework, music, and dance. Such skills attracted prospective husbands, if little else. It was not until the last part of the 19th century—with large-scale industrialization in the cities and the accompanying influx of relatively progressive European immigrants—that women were given basic educational opportunities.

Teacher training Normal or teacher-training schools were one option open to Brazilian women in the late 19th century. A diploma from a normal school allowed a woman to teach in a primary school. Women were not permitted to attend, much less teach, at institutions of higher learning until 1879.

A girl's education Normal schools were attended mostly by white girls, from respectable but needy families, who needed to contribute to the family income.

Girls of the lower classes often did not attend school at all. Upper-class girls were likely to go to expensive convent schools or be instructed by home tutors. Many upper-class parents believed that their daughters should be taught to be moral, virtuous, and pious creatures, and that it was not important to develop the girls' intellects. Women who wished to pursue higher education before 1879 found that they had to leave Brazil to get a college degree.

Maria Augusta Generosa Estrela The first Brazilian woman to become a doctor was Maria Augusta Generosa Estrela, who went to medical school in New York in 1875 at the age of 14.

While abroad, Maria Estrela was the

> "I hope to God that you will be here, Papa, on [the occasion of my graduation from medical school] to be the first to embrace and congratulate me on becoming the first Brazilian woman medical graduate.... Afterward, I shall return to our beloved and never forgotten Brazil—to cure, for free, all the poor, sick individuals of my sex...."
> —*Maria Estrela, in a letter to her father*

subject of many Brazilian newspaper articles. Many women considered her a heroine. When she returned to her hometown of Rio de Janeiro in 1882, she dedicated her medical practice to women and children.

School subjects taught After 1879, when girls were permitted to attend high schools, some women were able to enter the prestigious Colégio Dom Pedro II in Rio de Janeiro. Tuition fees were very high, and places were limited. More women were able to attend Rio's all-female Licue de Artes e Ofícios, but the curriculum there was decidedly feminine: music, drawing, and Portuguese were the only subjects.

In the normal schools, the courses for women included geography, history, gymnastics, and calligraphy, while at the Colégio, women received a classical education in Latin, Greek, and philosophy, among other subjects.

One 19th century Brazilian man claimed that women should not be given the vote because they "have functions that men do not; these functions are so sensitive, so delicate that the slightest nervous agitation, a fright, a moment of excitement, is sufficient to disturb them with consequences which many times are disastrous."

The first female graduates It was not until 1887, when Rita Lobato Velho Lopes graduated from medical school in Bahia, that a Brazilian woman received a degree from a Brazilian institution. In the late 1800s, Mirta de Campos became the first Brazilian woman to obtain a law degree from a Rio college.

Slow reform in attitudes Although some women followed in the footsteps of Rita Lobato and Mirta de Campos, many women were discouraged from higher education by their fathers and brothers. Many men believed that a professional life would ruin a woman's reputation and keep her from her husband and family. Even as late as 1924, the first Brazilian college in Rio de Janeiro had only 191 women out of 7,046 students. True educational reform—for males and females alike—did not come to most of the country until the 1930s.

The women's movement

Brazilian women first began advocating change in their society in the mid-19th century with the publication of journals written by and for women. These journals obviously had a very limited audience of literate women. Many of them were modeled on European women's journals and advocated that Brazilian society open itself up to the idea of progress. Women, they said, should be educated and allowed to participate in society in ways other than through mothering.

O Sexo Feminino (or *The Female Sex*), edited by Francisca Senhorinha da Motta Diniz of Minas Gerais, was first published in 1873.

Through the newspaper, Motta Diniz, a forthright teacher, aimed to "continually fight for the rights of our sex, which up to now have been trampled underfoot by the opposite sex." These early publications offered women the chance to express their opinions and exchange ideas.

Demands for suffrage After the fall of the monarchy in 1889, the women's rights movement in Brazil began to strengthen. Women began to demand the right to vote.

These early requests for women's suffrage were met with great opposition from Brazilian men. In 1891, the issue was debated in a congress but was not approved. Some male opponents felt

that women should not be full and equal members of society because they were biologically unable to deal with the fast pace of the outside world.

Expansion of women's horizons Women gained greater access to the world around them in the early 20th century. Some upper and middle-class urban women attended the movie theater regularly and even traveled on streetcars alone. They enjoyed participating in leisure activities such as tennis and swimming at Rio's famous beaches. They were influenced by images of life in America and Europe that they saw on the screen and in glossy women's magazines. They realized that women abroad had received the vote without losing their femininity or neglecting domestic responsibilities.

Brazilian women were given the right to vote in 1932, quelling the groundless fears of many men who felt that this kind of power would encourage women to abandon their first priority: home and family.

> "I am proposing the establishment of a league of Brazilian women. I am not proposing an association of 'suffragettes' who would break windows along the street, but, rather, of Brazilians who understand that a woman ought not to live parasitically based on her sex, taking advantage of man's animal instincts, but, rather, be useful, educate herself and her children, and become capable of performing those political responsibilities which the future cannot fail to allot her."
>
> —*Bertha Lutz, women's rights activist*

Many middle-class women led comfortable, leisurely lives as housewives. Others worked as dentists, pharmacists, typists, teachers, saleswomen, postal workers, and phone operators.

Women from the lower classes continued to be laundresses, domestic servants, and seamstresses. Many worked long hours in poorly lit, airless textile factories. Others were forced into prostitution. In the rural areas, however, women of all classes continued to live isolated lives.

The suffrage movement It was not until the second decade of the 20th century that the women's suffrage movement in Brazil began to make real progress in achieving its goal. Women were better educated and were able to organize themselves into associations for women's rights.

Brazilian advocates of women's rights were not radical absolutists who denounced femininity and sought a violent change in societal values. Rather, they were respectable, educated women from the upper and middle classes who, quietly and with dignity, hoped to achieve equality with Brazilian men. Many felt that women should be domestic creatures first and foremost, but that when they did enter the outside world, they should be paid what men were paid. They also wanted to be given equal opportunities for education.

Bertha Lutz, a biologist educated in Paris and holder of a law degree from a Brazilian institution, was the model women's rights activist. She became the most influential spokesperson for the women's suffrage movement.

Lutz's concerns Lutz sought educational and employment opportunities for women. She felt strongly that women should be able to hold important government positions, just as she herself did as secretary to Rio's National Museum. She helped found important Brazilian women's organizations, particularly the Brazilian Federation for the Advancement of Women (the Federação Brasileira pelo Progresso Feminino, or FBPF, as it was known), and represented the country in international women's conferences.

Women's suffrage in Latin America

Brazilian women were granted the right to vote considerably earlier than other Latin American women, as the following indicates. As a point of reference, nationwide suffrage was ratified in the United States in 1920.

Pre-World War II		Post-World War II	
Ecuador,	1929	Venezuela,	1947
Brazil,	1932	Argentina,	1947
Uruguay,	1932	Chile,	1949
Cuba,	1934	Haiti,	1950
		Bolivia,	1952
World War II		Mexico,	1953
El Salvador,	1939	Honduras,	1955
Dominican		Nicaragua,	1955
Republic,	1942	Peru,	1955
Panama,	1945	Colombia,	1957
Guatemala,	1945	Paraguay,	1961
Costa Rica,	1945		

Enfranchisement of Brazilian women In 1930, Brazil underwent a political revolution, and new, reform-minded leaders—including the clever politician, Getúlio Vargas—were installed. Lutz's FBPF, which had representatives in each Brazilian state, pressured the new government to hear its requests. In 1932, Lutz and her fellow suffragists finally achieved their goal, and Brazil became the second nation in Latin America to give women the right to vote.

A non-radical approach Brazilian feminists were successful because they were well-organized and careful not to threaten the workings of society by appearing too aggressive. They did not attempt to challenge the tenets of the Roman Catholic Church (though the Church had less of a hold in Brazilian society than elsewhere in Latin America), nor did they suggest that suffrage would encourage women to compete with men.

Within two years, a code of women's rights was formally adopted into the Brazilian constitution. Written by Lutz and Brazil's first female congresswoman, Carlota Pereira de Queiroz, the Thirteen Principles, as they were known, addressed issues such as maternity leave, equal employment and wage practices, and the right of women to hold public office.

Brazilian women after the vote

The political situation in Brazil following the success of women's suffrage was volatile. In 1937, President Vargas and his loyal military literally shut down the congress and suspended electoral privileges. Although Vargas had favored the women's movement initially, he gave women little support in the years that followed.

Between 1937 and 1945, when the Vargas dictatorship fell, neither women nor men were allowed to vote.

Suppression of rights Women also could not take jobs in government service. Brazilian women did not fare well in the 1950s under the presidency of Juscelino Kubitschek, who banned the FBPF. In 1964, after years of terrible inflation, social unrest, and the threat of communism, Brazil came under the rule of a repressive military dictatorship that was to last almost 20 years.

During military rule, the economy strengthened and the nation's urban centers were flooded with former agricultural workers looking for jobs in industry. The government censored the press, destroyed the democratic political system and suppressed its opposition, sometimes through human rights abuses. Meanwhile, the women's movement was forced to lie dormant.

Resurgence of women's issues In the 1970s and 1980s, women's organizations again found their voice, especially in the cities. A second era of feminism began. When Brazil's government began to liberalize, particularly in the mid 1970s, women's issues again came to the forefront. Women were still under-represented in government and other positions of power. They still were not paid equally, even when doing the same work men did. They continued to occupy traditional female roles in the family. However, more and more middle and upper-class women were attending college, and an increasing number of women were entering the work force, either by choice or out of necessity

A woman working in a hardware store.

A woman who lives in a *favela*.

Brazilian women today

It is impossible to describe the typical Brazilian woman unless both her class and her color are taken into account.

Upper and middle-class women In the 1980s and 1990s, Brazilian women of the upper classes have had access to the best education and the best jobs available. They have more freedom of choice—either to perform traditional roles within the home and not work or to enter the professions.

Young upper-class women are more likely to marry men who believe in the equality of the sexes, although there are Brazilian men from all classes who are still essentially macho in their outlook.

Middle-class women, however, have a much higher chance of marrying men who see a sharp difference in the roles of the sexes. Most middle-class Brazilian women work out of necessity, in jobs that are as various as those open to North American women.

Lower-class women Lower-class women—many of whom are black—have fared the least well in recent decades. The typical lower-class woman lives in a *favela* ("fah-VELL-ah"), a

shanty town with makeshift houses, found in all of Brazil's major cities. Her home often lacks indoor plumbing, and she must go to a communal well for water.

She raises her children, often with little help from her husband. At some time in her life, she has probably been the victim of some sort of domestic violence. Possibly, she has a job as a servant in the home of a middle or upper-class family and barely earns her livelihood. She probably cannot afford a wide variety of food and may receive inadequate medical care when she is sick. Her infants, due to improper pre-natal care, are less likely to live to their first birthdays than are the children of women of a higher social class.

The situation for poor women in Brazil today is bleak, but not hopeless. Women's groups have developed in many *favelas* in recent years, offering help in health, financial, and legal matters.

Women's groups aim to improve the lot of women in Brazil.

chapter three

Women in Society

n the last two decades, women's lives in Brazil have changed more than they have in the previous 100 years. The majority of Brazilian women today live in large cities. And, due to the country's current depressed economic situation, many of these women must work outside the home to contribute to the family income.

While in the early 20th century, it was unusual to find large numbers of women in the professions, today Brazil has many female doctors, lawyers, scientists, engineers, and politicians. There are also female environmentalists, police captains, and entrepreneurs who run their own advertising agencies and chemical companies. Middle-class women work as teachers in elementary and high schools. Women also dominate the field of social work, including organizations sponsored by the Catholic Church. Many Brazilian women excel in the arts. There are accomplished female singers, dancers, musicians, actresses, painters, sculptors, photographers, writers, and even several important film directors.

Unfortunately, the lives of poor women have not changed as drastically as those of women in the middle and upper classes. The economically disadvantaged Brazilian woman is still forced to earn a living through prostitution, factory work, and domestic service (the most common profession for women of her class). In this chapter, the lives of both ordinary and outstanding women will be examined.

Opposite: An anthropologist. While many women have made inroads into the professions, the poor, like this Bahian woman in Salvador (*right*), remain trapped in low-paid jobs.

Mary Helena Allegretti. In 1989, she received the Better World Society award for her work on environmental issues. She was also the recipient of a prestigious award from the United Nations Environment Program.

the environment. Brazilian women, such as black congresswoman Benedita da Silva and social worker Sonia Correa from Recife, participated in the meeting.

In recent years, women environmentalists in southern Brazil have been working to spread the word about the danger of using pesticides in agriculture. Within the *favelas*, women have spoken out against bad sanitation practices, unclean water, and poor garbage disposal.

Mary Helena Allegretti One Brazilian woman in particular has made strides toward helping preserve the Amazonian rain forests from being razed by enterprising cattle ranchers. For more than a decade, Mary Helena Allegretti, a former anthropologist, has been working with the native rubber-tappers in an attempt to improve their lives and conserve the forest that is their home.

Environmental movement

Brazil, with its vast natural resources and precious Amazonian rain forests, has received enormous attention in the last few years as environmental issues have become global concerns. In June of 1992, Rio de Janeiro hosted the Earth Summit, an international conference that brought together concerned individuals from all over the world to discuss a multitude of problems facing

> "My work in the Amazon is a very important experience in terms of Brazilian society.... My objective is to improve the conditions of life for those in the Amazon, but also to show Brazilian society that it is possible to change many things."
>
> —*Mary Helena Allegretti*
> *Brazilian environmentalist*

In 1980, Allegretti made a five-day river trip into the interior of Brazil that changed her life. The rubber-tappers whom she met were illiterate and lived at the mercy of the middlemen who "paid" for latex with food staples and refused to pay in currency. The tappers found themselves constantly in debt to the middlemen—a system Allegretti likened to slavery. She gave up a career in academia, moved to the country's interior and helped set up schools to teach the tappers to read and write and to protect themselves from being exploited.

While living in the Amazon, Allegretti also worked with Chico Mendes, a noted environmentalist who organized the tappers and small farmers to fight against cattle ranchers who wanted to destroy the land for pasture. Tragically, in 1988, Mendes was murdered by one such rancher who did not believe that peasants should have any say over the future of the land.

Since the murder, Allegretti and her cause have received international attention, and tens of thousands of acres of land have been designated official "reserves" that cannot be destroyed. (Rubber-tappers do not harm the trees they tap).

Allegretti works at the Institute for Amazonian Studies that she founded. She also deals with international environmental groups who are sympathetic to her cause.

Many poor black women, who have migrated from the impoverished northeast, work as maids.

Domestic service

Officially, more than three million women in Brazil are domestic servants, but the true number of women working as maids is closer to six million—a staggering 25% of the female work force.

A street vendor. Children from poor families are forced to become streetwise early in life.

typical monthly salary of a maid is only about $50—about 20% less than what the Brazilian government considers a living monthly wage. Some Brazilian social historians have likened the life of a maid to that of a black slave of the colonial era.

In Brazil, the typical maid works from before dawn to after dusk. If she lives in her own home, she often rises very early to get to work to serve breakfast. She comes home late, after she has cleaned up after dinner. If she lives with her employer, she often has a tiny room with no windows and little space for anything other than a bed. The room is usually just off the kitchen, where most of her work takes place.

For the live-in maid who has children of her own, life can be very difficult. During the week and maybe also on Saturday, she works for her employer, leaving her own children in the care of others if arrangements can be made. Many times, the children live on the streets, begging for food and searching garbage dumps for scraps. These children come home only occasionally.

Employing a maid Many middle and upper-class Brazilian women who have maids cannot conceive of life without them. The maids not only clean and cook for them, they act as full-time child care providers. In wealthier families, two or three maids might share these duties. The relationship between the woman

Wages and working life Domestic service, the most common type of employment for women in Brazil, is among the most poorly paid, not to mention the most labor intensive. The

of the house and her maid can be difficult on occasion.

Today many women who go out to work and leave their small children with the maid ex-perience tremendous feelings of guilt. They do not always wish to work outside the home, but to make ends meet they are forced to bring in a salary. The only way they can go to work, however, is to employ a maid to whom they need only pay a small amount.

Many women have wonderful, long-term relationships with their maids. They encourage their maids to go to school and improve themselves, even though they know they may lose them to more fulfilling work in the future. Others are constantly finding fault with their maids. They force them to work without days off or holiday leave.

Fighting for rights In the last few years, maids have begun to organize into unions to demand fair employment practices. In Rio de Janeiro and Recife, there are domestic employees' associations staffed by female lawyers who educate maids on their legal rights.

In the latest draft of the Brazilian constitution, maids are guaranteed the right to a minimum monthly salary, a day off each week, 30 days of paid annual leave, and paid maternity leave. Although many employers have yet to institute these practices, the lot of the maid now has hope for improvement.

"There is a saying in Brazil, 'When a husband and wife are fighting, you shouldn't stick your spoon in.' We feminists are saying the reverse: when domestic violence is going on, it has to do with all of us."
—*Brazilian feminist Jacqueline Pitanguy*

Brazil's all-female police stations

Domestic violence in Brazil is a problem facing women from all social classes, colors, and economic situations. According to "Update Brazil: Women's Police Stations," a Brazilian documentary about violence to women, nearly *half* of the adult women living in São Paulo, a city of 18 million, have been the victims of such crimes, a majority at the hands of a husband or boyfriend.

Help for abused women In 1985, the first all-female police station, staffed by women and dedicated to female victims, was opened in São Paulo. By 1992, there were 74 such women's police stations, or *delegacias* (dell-e-gah-SEE-yas) throughout the country, about 50 in the state of São Paulo and the rest distributed among other states. In 1985, the original station served more than 2,000 women. Presently, it serves almost four times that number.

> The new female police stations encourage women to be less afraid to report a crime and assure them that they will be treated sensitively when they do.

The need for redress Before the opening of the *delegacias*, a woman who had been beaten or raped often chose not to report such a crime to the authorities. If she did make a report, she was often turned away by male police officers who felt that domestic violence was an intimate problem that should be solved at home. Some officers even made the female victims feel that they were responsible for the violent treatment they received.

The *delegacias* have brought the crime of domestic violence out of the privacy of the home and into the public eye. They have made the problem a social rather than a personal one.

The women police officers who staff the *delegacias* receive the same training as male officers. They are put through the same rigorous exercises in self-defense and taught to use weapons. Some have also participated in special psychology courses directed at helping the victims of domestic violence. When a female victim makes a report at the station, several plainsclothes officers are sent to the scene of the crime, if the suspect is still considered dangerous. Sometimes, just a warning is issued; other times an arrest is made. The officers say that often the male suspects are surprised to see a female police officer, but that they do not often resist arrest. More often than not, however, the crime is passed on to an investigator and finally a lawyer who attempts to prosecute the offender.

Unfortunately, the tremendous backlog of cases makes it almost impossible for each case to be dealt with in a timely manner. As a result, very few offenders are actually brought to trial and put in jail. In a *delegacia* in São Luis, Maranhão, for instance, only 300 out of the 4,000 reports filed by women victims from 1988 to 1990 were handled by the courts, and only two men sent to prison. The *delegacias*, therefore, have succeeded more in offering female victims an immediate source of support for their problems than in punishing their offenders. If the Brazilian government continues its support, however, the number of convictions will increase.

Sports

In Brazil, as in nearly every country in Latin America, the national obsession is soccer—a sport played entirely by men. While some women are the greatest fans of their local or national soccer teams, they are rarely encouraged to don kneesocks or shorts and run on the field to participate. Sports with any type of physical contact are frequently off limits to Brazilian women, so women are

usually linked with traditionally feminine and non-violent sports and leisure pastimes such as swimming, gymnastics, tennis, horseback riding, and aerobics. Opportunities for most of these activities are often limited to private clubs and therefore available only to those who can afford the expensive dues.

"Dental floss" bikinis Brazilians usually spend a good deal of time at the beach, if they live near the coast. *Carioca* ("car-ree-AW-ca") women (women from Rio de Janeiro) in particular have achieved a kind of international fame for the tiny bikinis (nicknamed "dental floss") they wear at the beach.

Songwriter Tom Jobim forever immortalized (and stereotyped) female beachgoers with the lyrics to his song "The Girl from Ipanema": "Tall and tan and young and lovely, the girl from Ipanema goes walking, and when she passes, each one she passes, goes 'ahhh.'"

Basketball In terms of competitive amateur sports, some Brazilian women athletes have managed to break through gender barriers. Most of these play for the Brazilian women's basketball team. The team participated, for the first time, in the 1992 Olympics in Barcelona. The Brazilian team was led by two female stars who are so talented that they are not permitted to play on the same team when competing at the state level.

A favorite pastime of many Brazilian women is relaxing on the beach.

Hortência's story Born in the town of Potirandaba into a very poor family, Hortência discovered her athletic talent at a young age. She originally played handball and ran track and field. At 13, she gave up running because she found it too lonely and started playing basketball, even though people discouraged her from taking up what Brazilians usually consider a masculine sport. "People told me, 'you'll get too many muscles,'" she said, "I'm proud of my muscles, I put them there." She learned that "you have to compete not with men but with yourself, and do the things you like."

Now Hortência plays for the state of São Paulo, where she often scores as many as 35 to 40 points a game. She is the captain of the national team. Once she broke a Brazilian record by scoring 64 points in a single game.

In the 1991 Pan American Games, she led the Brazilian team to an astounding victory over the United States, which until then had sustained a 42-game, decade-long winning streak. Although the Brazilians were behind 26-8 at one point in the game, they ended up defeating the Americans 87-84. Their coach, Maria Cardoso, used excellent strategy throughout the game, allowing Hortência and Paula to take turns playing and resting early in the game, and using the two stars together during the last exciting minutes.

To make Hortência's Cinderella

Hortência (right), participating in the women's basketball competition at the Pan American games in Indianapolis, Indiana on August 17, 1987.

Two female stars In Brazil, they are known by only their first names: Paula and Hortência. Paula is Maria Paula da Silva, a 32-year-old guard who also plays professional basketball in Spain. Thirty-three-year-old Hortência de Fatima Marcari Oliva, also a guard, is Brazil's superstar player, with a rags-to-riches life story that sounds a little like Cinderella's.

story complete, she is also beautiful, hard-working (she practices nearly 10 hours a day), and generous. In 1989, she married one of Brazil's most successful nightclub owners, José Victor Oliva. Soccer star Pelé was one of the groomsmen at their wedding.

In the 1990 season, Hortência played in Italy as well as Brazil and earned nearly $200,000 that year. During the halftime sessions in Brazil, she is surrounded by children.

Teaching

Although there are presently more women attending Brazilian colleges than men, college classes are taught mostly by men. Teaching at the pre-school, elementary, and high school levels, on the other hand, is truly a female occupation. Women make up 98% of nursery school teachers, 87% of elementary school teachers, and 53% of high school teachers. Only about 21% of college professors are women.

Although teaching has been a respected means of employment for women in Brazil since the 19th century, it is still an underpaid profession.

The teaching experience A day in the life of a public school teacher in a large Brazilian city sounds much like a day in the life of an American teacher in an inner-city school. In both countries, there are often too many students in a class and few teaching aids. There is

The standards for public school teachers in Brazil are generally not as high as they are in other countries, possibly because there are so many teaching positions to fill and so few people who can afford to work for less than $200 a month (for two shifts). Only about 37% of Brazilian teachers have a college degree; another 41% completed high school and a one-year teacher training program. However, more than 13% of teachers have not completed their elementary education. Some teachers try to go to school at night to work toward a degree. Others simply cannot find the time or the funds.

some violence in and around the classroom. One essential difference in Brazil, however, is that some of the most crowded public schools operate on as many as five shifts a day. The schools are open from about seven in the morning to as late as eleven at night. Teachers work for one or two shifts and then go on to another job that probably pays them more. The typical shift lasts about four hours. Subjects include Portuguese, mathematics, social studies, and science.

Private schools Teaching at a private school is a different experience. Nearly all Brazilian children from the middle and upper classes attend private schools. In São Paulo alone, there are 928 private schools, as compared to only 672 public schools.

The *lambada*. Brazilians are known the world over for their ability to express themselves in song and dance.

hurry in an effort to make way for the next shift.

Music and dance

The word Brazil is virtually synonymous with music and dance. Musical styles such as the famous samba, bossa nova (a mixture of Brazilian samba and North American jazz), and *tropicalismo* (a combination of rock and traditional African-Brazilian music) come from Brazil, as does the bawdy dance step called the *lambada*.

Stores selling musical instruments can be found on Rio de Janeiro's fanciest shopping streets next to elegant boutiques and trendy restaurants. On any given day, the beaches are packed with sunbathers dancing to live music provided by bands giving impromptu concerts.

Brazilian women have been active leaders and participants in the musical field for many decades. Magda Tagliaferro, who died in her 90s in 1986, was a world renowned classical pianist for more than 50 years. Samba singer Alcione, one of Brazil's hottest stars, and pop singer Simone, a former basketball player, have begun to make international names for themselves. And jazz singer Leny Andrade has been called the Brazilian Sarah Vaughan. Here are some famous female singers and musicians.

Nara Leão During her lifetime, Nara Leão was called the most important

Better conditions Many private schools are run by the Catholic Church. Classrooms are clean and equipped with all the necessary aids. Teachers are paid higher salaries and need not take other jobs to supplement their incomes. They are also able to cover subjects more thoroughly because they do not have to

female singer of bossa nova and *tropicalismo*. She grew up in a home where musicians gathered and began playing the guitar seriously at age 11. In the late 1960s, Leão left Brazil for Paris in protest of the harsh military dictatorship that had taken over her country. She returned to Brazil in 1971. She achieved international fame before dying of a brain tumor in 1989 at the age of 47.

Bidù Sayão Born in Rio de Janeiro in 1902, Bidù Sayão left Brazil at an early age to study opera in France. In 1936, she sang at New York's Carnegie Hall. The following year, she sang with the world-famous Metropolitan Opera. Sayão's renditions of classic roles—Mimi in *La Bohème*, Violetta in *La Traviata*—were highly polished and memorable. In 1986 she was honored in New York for the 50th anniversary of her operatic debut at the Met.

Gal Costa One of the orginal Bahian tropicalistas, Gal Costa has since expanded her style to include soul, folk, jazz, and rock. She is one of the most popular recording stars in Brazil today. Although Costa sings only in Portuguese, her style is so appealing that she can be appreciated by speakers of any language.

Nara Leão. On one popular album, she sang American songs like Judy Garland's "Over the Rainbow" and "Tea for Two" in Portuguese, and the effect was refreshing. According to a Brazilian music critic, Leão was able to "rescue the listener from the hell of the contemporary world" with her fine voice.

Samba singer
Elza Soares.

sounds of bossa nova toward a more traditional folk style, and *tropicalismo* was born. Many of Bethânia's albums are extremely popular in Europe and in Latin American countries other than Brazil, and she is starting to build a reputation in the United States.

Beth Carvalho She is not a typical Brazilian samba singer. Samba, the throbbing music of Brazilian carnival, was originally the art form of poor uneducated blacks living in urban *favelas*. Carvalho is an upper-class white woman whose talent knows no social or economic boundaries; her samba records sell to both rich and poor. She sings with Rio's most famous samba school, Mangueira, and feels very strongly for the plight of black Brazilians although, being an upper-class white woman, she lives totally outside their society. To her, samba is a joyous music as well as a "lament," a form of black resistance.

Elza Soares Like Beth Carvalho, Elza Soares is a samba specialist. Born into a poor family, Soares has been tremendously successful in her career and has made more than 300 albums. Her voice has been compared to Louis Armstrong's and her energy level to Tina Turner's. She also has a remarkable ability to mimic musical instruments such as the guitar, the sax, and certain percussion instruments. Her concerts are said to be dramatic and soulful.

Maria Bethânia Considered the supreme Brazilian folksinger, Maria Bethânia has been likened to Edith Piaf of France and Americans Judy Garland and Billie Holiday. Her deep, throaty voice is haunting and full of spirituality. With Gal Costa, singer Gilberto Gil, and her brother, Caetano Veloso, Bethânia revolutionized Brazilian music in the 1960s, steering it away from the cool

The spectacle of Brazilian Carnival

The Carnival in Rio de Janeiro is one of the world's most exuberant, spectacular, brilliantly colorful, and stunning festivals. On this occasion, *cariocas* act out their wildest fantasies. They forget their place in society, their money problems, their nine-to-five jobs, and immerse themselves in this pre-Lenten celebration by dancing in the streets or at a fancy ball until dawn, dressed in tiny sequinned bikinis or richly embroidered colonial-style costumes. On the Sunday and Monday before Ash Wednesday, nearly 100,000 people fill the Sambadrome to watch the highlight of Carnival: the parade of the samba schools. Some 65 million people in Brazil and around the world watch the event on television and speculate on which samba school or neighborhood organization will win first prize for the most elaborate float, the most imaginative costumes, and the most memorable theme song.

For four days every February or March, Brazilians celebrate Carnival. Traditonally, it starts the Sunday before the beginning of Lent and ends on Ash Wednesday, although the festivities normally extend to at least a week. Carnival is an event—a riot of music, dance, and drink before the abstinence of Lent. It represents a release of energy, an affirmation of freedom, an expression of hope, a belief in life itself. For black Brazilians especially, it symbolizes freedom from oppression and the will to live.

Brazilian Carnival

Women are very much a part of Carnival, as spectators and as participants. Within the samba schools, which are usually located in poor black neighborhoods or *favelas* and have as many as 4,000 regular members, women are often in charge of helping to design and sew all the costumes worn during the Carnival. During the last few weeks before Carnival, these seamstresses work day and night to complete the costumes.

During the Carnival, it is traditional for each samba school to have an entire group of women dressed like *baianas* ("BUY-yahn-ahs"), or women from Bahia, the birthplace of Carnival, marching near the school's float. And, atop each float are found scores of scantily clad female dancers led by a beautiful flag-bearer, the most significant woman in the school. The women on the floats are always *mulatas*, or women of mixed race. In Brazil, the *mulata* is representative of the mixing of the races that created Brazil; she is also a symbol of raw sexuality and eroticism.

Thematic approach Each samba school spends an entire year preparing for Carnival. First, a theme is selected that will be carried out in the design of the float, the costumes, and the choice of music and lyrics for the school's song. The theme can be based on an historical event, such as the abolition of slavery or a current social problem. One year, a samba school called Beija-Flor (which means "hummingbird") opened the parade with a group of men dressed in tattered clothes like beggars. Floats may also carry enormous monsters, giant replicas of unpopular politicians, fountains with scented water, and realistic scenes of *favela* life.

Samba was originally the art form of poor uneducated blacks living in urban *favelas*. In 1991, a famous samba school called Mangueira used "The Three Lacemakers of the Universe" for their theme. Lacemaking is a Bahian art, and the three lacemakers were represented by the sky, the sea, and the earth. In 1988, the same school honored an historical place called Palmares, a 19th-century community of slaves who had revolted against their masters. The leader of Palmares was a black man

named Zumbi, and Mangueira's song that year went like this: "I dreamt of Zumbi of Palmares' return...that the sadness of blacks was over...."

A lavish celebration Carnival is still primarily a festival of disadvantaged blacks who save all year for their extravagant costumes. Costumes and materials for floats are also partially subsidized by celebrities, like samba singer Alcione, soap opera stars, and even groups of Mafia-like gangsters who contribute money from the illegal lottery-like games they run.

Lately, Rio de Janeiro's Carnival has been infiltrated by members of the middle and upper classes who join samba schools so they too can parade in the Sambadrome. To many, this represents the razing of barriers between races and social classes in Brazil. To others, it means that Carnival is on its way to becoming just another amusement of the rich, instead of a once-a-year fantasy for the poor.

Brazilians spare no expense in dressing up for Carnival, which has succeeded in attracting people of all races and social classes.

According to Alma Guiller-moprieto, who joined Mangueira for a year to write *Samba*, a remarkable, intimate account of life in a samba school, to dance the samba properly you must give the impression that "somebody is moving like crazy from the waist down while an entirely different person is observing the pro-ceedings from the waist up....If you are a woman," she continues, "you should practice with a book on your head. Twelve hip beats per minute will look like a hundred if you're wearing sequins."

A housewife tuning in to a soap opera

Soap operas

Brazilian television soap operas, called *novelas* ("no-VELL-ahs"), have a significant effect on the socety as a whole, particularly among women.

Like the American nighttime soap operas such as "Dallas" and "Dynasty," the Brazilian *novelas* are dramatic tales of the lives of a host of interesting characters. When the nation is in the grip of a good *novela*, more than 90% of the possible viewing audience tunes in, leaving the local bars and stores empty.

In Brazil, the *novela*-watching audience—made up of men and women from every race and social group—can be 70 million strong on any given night. The Brazilian *novelas* are so well produced that they have been exported to more than 40 countries in Europe, Asia, and Latin America.

In Brazil, *novelas* are more than television fantasies about powerful, greedy people who have little in common with their viewing audience. By presenting a picture of Brazilian society, past or present, they not only entertain but also carry social or political messages.

Popular novelas One extremely popular *novela* shown in the mid-1980s is "Roque Santeiro" (or "The Saint-Maker"), which takes place in a small rural place called Misery Town, where the politicians are corrupt, the macho husbands cheat on their wives, and the supposed "saint" of the title is a common thief. Called "a mirror of Brazilian society," "Roque Santeiro" deals with such important issues as gender roles, land reform, the gap between rich and poor, and the role of the Catholic Church in society.

One *novela* that featured a powerful woman character is "The Slave Isaura," a tale of a slave girl who fought for the abolition of slavery in the 1880s. Actress Lucélia Santos, who played the title role, was accosted by excited fans when she visited China. The series had been dubbed and shown there.

Movies

Brazilian filmmaking is dominated by men, with a few notable exceptions. Although a handful of women directed and produced movies in the 1920s and 1930s in Brazil, the medium did not truly open up to women until the 1970s when women began making television shows and short documentaries. In the 1980s and 1990s, a few female directors began creating feature films.

Tisuka Yamasaki Japanese-Brazilian Tisuka Yamasaki made *Gaijín, Roads to Freedom* in 1980. The word "Gaijín" is Japanese for foreigner. Yamasaki's film concerns a Japanese family that emigrated to Brazil in the early 1900s and must confront life in a profoundly different culture.

In 1983, she made a movie about a

> **"My film ['Hour of the Star'] is not a feminist film; it's a feminine film."**
> —*Brazilian film director Suzana Amaral*

woman's sexuality called *Parahyba, a Macho Woman*. Two years later, she turned to a political theme with *Beloved Motherland*.

Suzana Amaral Suzana Amaral, director of the award-winning film adaptation of Clarice Lispector's novel *Hour of the Star* (see Chapter 5) began her feature film career when she was in her 50s and had finished raising nine children. *Hour of the Star* tells the story of a poor and very ordinary young girl (played by the accomplished Brazilian actress Marcelia Cartaxo) who comes to São Paulo to find work. It is a moving, sensitive film that provides great insight into the Brazilian woman's urban experience.

In 1986, it was nominated for Best Foreign Film by the American Academy of Motion Picture Arts and Sciences. The film also won many awards that year in the Berlin Film Festival. It won every conceivable award in Brazil the year it was released, ran for six solid months at a theater in São Paulo and received a five-minute standing ovation after it was shown at a film festival in Brasília.

The lace-making techniques practiced by women in the northeast were originally brought to Brazil by Portuguese colonists in the 17th century.

the tourist market, they were formerly used as a kind of visual aid to teach children about the miracle of life. Sometimes the artisan makes a single pregnant figure; other times she creates an entire scene, complete with a woman in the midst of giving birth surrounded by female attendants such as a midwife and her helpers. The clay figures are about a foot tall and painted with simple geometric designs.

The Karajo and members of other Amazonian tribes display their work in a government-sponsored shop in Belém that sells jewelry, wood carvings, baskets, and ceramic pieces.

Crafts

In Brazil, as in many Latin American cultures, women were the primary craft makers for centuries. In pre-colonial Brazil, tribal women were responsible for the creation of utilitarian pottery, rugs, and garments. Many beautiful crafts are still being made by Brazilian women. Other craft-making methods have had to be relearned because they were forgotten in the face of 20th-century technology.

Clay dolls Women of the Karajo tribe of the Amazon currently craft what are known as "birthing dolls" out of clay. Although these figures are now sold to

Bahian lace-making The black women of Bahia are famous for their elegant handmade lace. Although some of their pieces are sold to tourists, most are purchased by Brazilian women who wear them for *candomblé* or African religious rites and celebrations.

Today the lace-making trade is stronger in Bahia than in Portugal and the rest of Europe. Entire shops are devoted to the craft. If you walk around the city of Salvador, you may see women making lace on their front porches. A large piece of lace, for a tablecloth for instance, can take months of painstaking work.

Handmade rugs In the region around Diamantina, a former gold and diamond mining town in the interior state of

Minas Gerais, about 2,000 women make magnificent handmade rugs that are sold by an artisan's cooperative. The rugs, named after the village in Portugal where the style originated, are known around the world for their intricate patterns and tight weave.

Many of the women in the cooperative work in their homes so that they can keep an eye on the children and earn a steady income at the same time. The cooperative offers them good medical care, a day-care center, and provides them with a pet goat from which they get a half-gallon of milk a day for their families. Some weavers even live in homes provided by the cooperative. Each square yard of rug woven by the women requires about 72,000 individual stitches. The best weavers produce about eight such yards of cloth per month.

Tapestry work. Some of the cherished techniques of traditional crafts were passed down from mother to daughter over hundreds of years.

Women participating in an anti-violence demonstration in Rio de Janeiro.

Deputies is made up of women, and there is only one woman in the Senate. There are women mayors, however, in both rural and urban areas, including the nation's largest city, São Paulo. In 1990, the first female cabinet minister was appointed.

Women's groups and social change
Throughout the last three decades, women have organized themselves into many types of organizations to strive for social change. In many instances they have been quite effective in having their demands answered.

In the 1960s and 70s, women created housewives' associations and mothers' clubs in poor neighborhoods to push for more day-care centers and better health care. During Brazil's military regime, middle-class women organized themselves to fight for educational opportunities for their children and the stabilization of food prices. They also were a major force behind the human rights movement. In 1988, women living in the Santa Marta *favela* built a day-care center for nearly 70 children with their own hands.

Currently, there are more than 400 feminist groups in Brazil dealing with such issues as equal work for equal pay, family planning, and violence against women. Feminist lawyers also helped draft a new Married Women's Statute in 1988 to be included in the new constitution.

Politics

Although Brazil was the second nation in Latin America to grant the vote to women and women make up more than half of the voting population, the country has had few female political leaders.

Only about 6% of the Chamber of

Mayor of São Paulo

In 1988, a majority of the citizens of São Paulo, Brazil's largest city, shocked the nation by electing a woman to the prominent position of mayor. Before the election, Luiza Erundina de Souza seemed an unlikely candidate, and not just because she is a woman. De Souza grew up in the impoverished northeast—an area considered a rural backwater by many urban Brazilians—where her father made saddles. In addition, she is a Marxist and a member of the leftist Workers' Party. She does not fit the description of the typical Brazilian woman.

When she first took office, she was constantly being ridiculed by the Brazilian press who did not feel she could tackle the city's terrible economic and social problems. By her third year in office, de Souza was making excellent progress in getting the city under control. She helped decrease São Paulo's financial debt, authorized the construction of thousands of public housing units, as well as many hospitals, day-care centers, and schools. She also dramatically increased the number of public buses, raised the salaries of city workers (while cutting her own) and established laundry and food service facilities in poverty-stricken neighborhoods. Helping the poor is one of her primary concerns, and she has consistently opted for self-help programs over outright donations.

De Souza is now in her mid-50s and has remained single. She still has some critics, but most *paulistas* ("POW-lee-stahs"), or residents of São Paulo, admire her excellent administrative skills, her honesty, and the fact that she keeps her promises.

Zélia Cardosa de Mello. She resigned from her post as Minister of the Economy because of her love affair with another cabinet minister.

Zélia Cardoso de Mello In 1990, President Fernando Collor de Mello appointed Zélia Cardoso de Mello (no relation) to one of Brazil's most powerful governmental positions, Minister of the Economy. For the 14 months that she held office, Zélia was in charge of Brazil's major banks as well as the national treasury. She was faced with the daunting task of getting the world's sixth largest economy under control by lowering the enormous federal deficit and keeping inflation at a minimum.

Before she could make any real progress, Zélia resigned her post because of a public scandal. During her tenure, the never-married Zélia was having an affair with Bernardo Cabral, the Minister of Justice, who had been married for 30 years.

A few months after her resignation, *Zélia, a Passion*, an intimate account of the affair (written by Fernando Sabino with Zélia's permission), hit the bookstores in Brazil and became an immediate bestseller. In the book, readers learn about the love notes the two ministers passed during cabinet meetings, as well as Cabral's empty promises to leave his wife, a traditional woman who, according to the book, "only appeared in the living room to serve coffee or food."

Brazilian feminists were both appalled that a role model could confess about her personal life so publicly, and proud of her for bringing Cabral's dishonesty and her own pain to the attention of all Brazilians. Cabral, who was also forced to resign his post, says he is planning to write his own memoirs telling the real story of the affair. Zélia, meanwhile, has established her own economics research company and is planning to re-enter the world of politics.

Women and the Catholic Church

The Catholic Church has been a force in Brazilian society since the first years of colonialism. For hundreds of years, Brazilian women have been entering the convent, either, as in the past, to find shelter from the opposite sex, or to take vows to devote their lives to serving God. The leadership of the Church has always been in the hands of men as women are not permitted to be priests.

A nun's vocation Up until quite recently, most Brazilian nuns were either administrators and teachers in private Catholic schools, established to educate the children of the middle and upper classes, or they ran Catholic hospitals. Today, however, many nuns have changed the course of their lives by deciding to dedicate themselves to helping the poor, especially those living in the arid rural areas of Brazil's northeast.

Other nuns have begun what are called Christian base communities in poor urban areas. These grassroot organizations, with mostly female members, serve to organize *favela* dwellers to fight for better housing, cleaner water, and adequate education.

Remembering the forgotten Daphne Patai, the author of *Brazilian Women Speak*, interviewed Brazilian women from all walks of life. One of her interviewees, Sister Denise (not her real name) had given up the security of the convent to live among poor Brazilians.

When Sister Denise moved to the northeast and lived among the poor for some time, she realized that the Church must learn from the poor how to help them help themselves.

Sister Denise called her poor neighbors "those people who live marginalized lives, those people who are actually forgotten by society, who are humanity's leftovers."

Sister Dulce One particularly selfless nun who devoted her life to helping the poor of Bahia was Sister Dulce. Her acts of charity so touched the hearts of others that she was called the "Good Angel of Bahia," Sister Dulce was an international figure. She was nominated for the Nobel Peace Prize several times and received a personal visit from the Pope during his last tour of Brazil.

Sister Dulce grew up in Bahia, and until she entered the convent in 1932, led the life of a normal girl—playing with her girlfriends in the streets and cheering avidly for the local soccer team. Her life's work was the Hospital of Santo Antônio in Bahia, which she ran for more than 30 years. The hospital accommodates nearly 900 needy patients.

Up until the last days of her life, Sister Dulce was struggling to raise money to build new housing for the 130 orphans who live in the hospital. She died in March 1992, at the age of 77.

Literature

Today Brazil has many outstanding female writers who tell their stories through fact or fiction.

Brazil has its share of women's magazines, including mainstream consumer publications such as *Claudia*, and feminist journals. There are radio programs and television shows with female hosts, some dedicated to women's issues, as well as prominent newspapers that employ female journalists.

Scholars of Brazilian women's history have lamented the fact that so few women of the past left behind any written records to be studied by today's historians. Because so few women could read and write before the 20th century, the absence of personal letters, diaries, and works of poetry or fiction is not surprising.

Alice Brant One of the few women who did leave a record of life in the late 1800s was Alice Brant. Born in Diamantina, she kept a diary from 1893 to 1895, when she was between the ages of 12 and 15. In 1957, it was translated by poet Elizabeth Bishop and published under the title *The Diary of "Helena Morley,"* (a pseudonym chosen by Brant).

The diary provides a vivid picture of a young girl's life in a poor rural area with strong patriarchal traditions. "Helena," who was fortunate enough to attend a teacher's training or normal school, was articulate about how she spent her days doing the washing, taking river baths, preparing food, going to school, following Church rituals, and conversing with her grandmother.

Carolina Maria de Jesus In recent times, another woman has also written a book in the form of a diary. Carolina Maria de Jesus's book, *Child of the Dark*, was published in 1960. It offers a portrait of life in Brazil from the point of view of a poor black woman living in an urban *favela*. A brief account of de Jesus's life in a *favela* and how she came to publish her book is in Chapter 4.

Like Alice Brant's book, her book is eloquent in its simplicity. *Child of the Dark*, however, offers a much bleaker view of society because the terrible struggles the writer recounts are still taking place in Brazil's overcrowded cities.

Fiction writers In the last two decades in particular, Brazilian female fiction writers have been especially prolific.

In general, the themes that these female novelists deal with include politics, death, the family, female sexuality, and the changing roles of women.

Carolina Maria de Jesus, who wrote about life in a *favela*.

Alice Brant describes her mother

Alice Brant was excellent at transcribing entire conversations and spent a good amount of time pondering the difficult life of women, as the following excerpt illustrates:

"Papa is much beloved in my family. Everybody likes him and says he's a very good man and a very good husband. I like hearing it but I'm always surprised at their just saying that papa's a good husband and never saying that mama's a good wife....With papa leading a miner's life, most of the money he gets goes back into mining; there's not much left over for the house. We complain about things sometimes, but never a peep from mama. She never says a word that might upset my father; she just keeps telling him: 'Don't be discouraged; to live is to suffer. God will help us.'...When I see mama getting up at five in the morning, going out in the yard in all this cold, struggling with wet, green wood to start the kitchen fire to have our coffee and porridge ready by six, I feel so sorry I could die. She begins then and goes without stopping until evening, when we sit on the sofa in the parlor....And yet nobody ever says mama's a good wife...."

Wednesday, July 10th, 1895

Clarice Lispector was a notable existentialist writer who had won several literary prizes. Her work is seen as extraordinarily innovative, her writing style poetic, and her themes on marriage and infidelity brilliantly probed. There is a profile of her in Chapter 5.

Nélida Piñon is a novelist and short story writer who is also one of the few female members of the Brazilian Academy of Letters. Born in 1937 of a Spanish father and a Brazilian mother, she worked as a journalist and then an assistant editor of a literary magazine, *Cadernos Brasileiros*. She also taught college courses in Brazil and at Columbia University in New York.

In 1955, she became a full-time author. She has published more than six novels and three collections of short stories. Several of her works have won literary prizes and have been translated into Spanish, French, English, and Polish.

Nélida Piñon. She is probably the most respected female writer in Brazil today.

chapter four

Being Woman

razil is one of the most racially diverse countries in the world. About half of Brazil's 140 million people are of mixed race, and there are more blacks in Brazil than in any nation outside of Africa. Brazil also has its share of Asians, especially Japanese, as well as people of German, Italian, and pure Portuguese ancestry. There are also some 200,000 Brazilians of Indian heritage. During the last census, statisticians recorded more than 100 different terms used by Brazilians to describe their skin tones and facial features. Within the same family, the mother can have light brown skin, one daughter white skin, and another black.

However integrated the society appears, it is certainly not free of racial prejudice. Black people, and black women in particular, occupy the lowest rung of the social and economic ladder. Despite the powerlessness of Brazilian blacks as a whole, they have a reputation for being the nation's cultural guardians. Through their religion, art and cuisine, they have kept in close touch with their African roots, especially in the primarily black state of Bahia.

In the last several decades, the overwhelming majority of Brazilians have become urban dwellers. Within the cities and the towns, there is a sharp distinction between the rich and the poor, the landowners and the landless, the educated and the uneducated. The gap between rich and poor is widening as the country becomes more and more mired in debt, unemployment, and inflation.

Brazilian women belong to different ethnic groups, from the black *(opposite)* to the white *(right)* to those of mixed blood.

A young woman of mixed ancestry from Recife.

The race question

For generations Brazil is described as a country of racial harmony, where people of an extraordinary range of colors live side by side with no discrimination and no violence. Some of that idealization of Brazilian society is true. Brazilian culture was indeed born when the Portuguese settlers mixed their blood with that of native Indians and black slaves. Brazilians are generally more willing to accept color differences due to their mixed heritage. There is no legal racial discrimination in Brazil as there is in South Africa, and large-scale violent clashes between races are rare.

Harder life for blacks Racial discrimination, however, manifests itself in Brazil in insidious ways. When the statistics are examined, it is evident that black Brazilians do not generally participate in the middle and upper echelons of society and, therefore, reap few of the benefits. Consider the following.

- The life expectancy of a black person in Brazil is eight years less than that of a white person.
- A black child is much more likely to die before the age of five than a white child due to poor living conditions and inadequate health care.

- Sixty percent of the people living a sub-standard existence are black.
- In São Paulo and Recife, a black doctor makes about 22% less than a white doctor; a black secretary makes 40% less than a white one;
- In the northeast, a white manual laborer earns 50% more than a black one.
- The illiteracy rate among blacks is 33% compared to 15% for whites.
- Eighty percent of the people in Brazil's prisons are black.
- There are very few blacks on television, either in advertisements or elsewhere. Those who do appear are often cast as athletes, maids, or criminals.
- The diet of a black slave was higher in protein and calories than that of a black person today.

In addition, many jobs are closed to blacks, although this practice is illegal. Some advertisements for jobs require the applicant to be "of good appearance," that is, with white or light skin. There are few blacks found in colleges or in upper-level positions in business, government and the military. Even in Salvador de Bahia, which is 80% black and mulatto, nearly all the members of the city council are white.

In some fancy apartment buildings, blacks are required to use special service elevators, and some clubs make it mandatory for black nannies to wear uniforms.

A black awareness movement has sprung up. Black leaders are encouraging publishers to rewrite school textbooks to take into account the black slave experience. On May 13, 1988, the 100th anniversary of the abolition of slavery, many blacks protested the festivities, claiming that little had changed for blacks in the past century.

Racial terms

Although today some 90% of couples in Brazil are of the same race, the country was populated by the intermingling of three distinct races (European, Indian and African), and most Brazilians have some mixed blood. Here are some of the terms Brazilians use to describe their various ethnic makeups and skin colors:

branco: white skin, which applies to people of European (Portuguese, German) heritage;

amarelo: yellow skin, which applies to people of Asian heritage;

moreno: brown skin;

moreno claro: light brown skin;

acastanhado: chestnut-colored skin;

mulato: dark brown skin; also, a person born to a white parent and a black parent;

caboclo: a person born to a white parent and an Indian parent;

mameluco: a person born to a black parent and an Indian parent.

"[Blacks] have gone from the hold of the ship to the basements of society."
—*Zézé Motta, black actress*

> "The Brazilian soul emerged from the confrontation between Portuguese melancholy and African *joie de vivre*. The Portuguese are pessimists, full of doubts and preoccupied with death. Africans exude life, are at ease with themselves physically and with nature and know how to laugh, celebrate and enjoy themselves. They brought a rhythm and a vital energy to the new culture which are immediately recognizable. If you hear Brazilian music or watch a Brazilian dance, you will see it straight away."
>
> —*Brazilian writer Jorge Amado*

Color prejudices While many blacks in Brazil have an increased sense of pride in their heritage, many others subscribe to the myth that "whiter is better." Consider the popularity of Xuxa, the blond, blue-eyed television star (see Chapter 5), who is worshiped by millions of dark, brown-eyed children.

Furthermore, during the last census, statistics were skewed because millions of people claimed that their skin was lighter than it actually was. For many Brazilians, the word black is synonymous with a host of negative images like poverty, ignorance, and crime. White, on the other hand, stands for beauty, wealth, and opportunity.

The African spirit of Brazil

Black Brazilians, descended from the 3 to 4 million black slaves brought from Africa, have contributed a great deal to Brazilian society.

Throughout Brazil, blacks are the main creators of and participants in the annual celebration of Carnival. The words samba and *lambada* are derived from the African language. Many black Brazilians are famous for their talents in music and dance. African-Brazilian food is enjoyed throughout Brazil, and African-Brazilian religions are adopted by Brazilians of all races.

The center of black Brazil is Salvador de Bahia (known simply as Bahia), the oldest city in the country. Some 20,000 of the city's nearly 100,000 buildings are more than 250 years old. Most were built using slave labor.

Blacks and people of mixed race represent some 80% of the 2.5 million people in Bahia. Many of them feel that Bahian life is freer from racial discrimination than other cities. Bahia is the home of African-Brazilian art, poetry, *candomblé* (an African-Brazilian religion), music, dance, clothing, cuisine, and the black awareness movement. It is proudly known as Africa do Sul—the Africa of South America.

The Bahian woman She has great presence in Bahia. She wears clothing reminiscent of her African heritage: a full, tiered white skirt and a brightly colored off-the-shoulder blouse, or a lacy outfit suggestive of that worn in a *candomblé* ritual. Her signature is her turban, also of vivid colors, twisted and wrapped around her head, and accompanied by large hoop earrings.

The female Bahian street vendor is a fixture on the sidewalks and beaches of Bahia. Over a small portable grill, she prepares spicy fritters made from pea flour stuffed with flavorful dried shrimp. Bahian women also work in craft shops selling handmade lace and jewelry.

Religion

According to the last census figures, more than 90% of Brazilians consider themselves Roman Catholic. Brazil is, in fact, the largest Catholic country in the world.

The Catholic Church is a strong force among some communities in Brazil, but it does not seem to influence the population as much as it does in other Latin American countries. People perform Catholic rituals on important occasions—baptism, first communion, weddings, and funerals—but they are unlikely to be avid followers of their religion on a day-to-day basis.

A Bahian woman dressed in distinctive clothing that reflects her African heritage.

Candomblé Although many people claim to be Catholics on paper, many Brazilians of all races and classes are also followers of African-Brazilian cults. The oldest such religion in Brazil is called *candomblé*, which makes its home in Bahia. Bahia may have hundreds of historic Catholic churches, but it also has thousands of *candomblé* temples.

Candomblé was developed by black slaves who were forced to adopt the Catholic religion when they reached Brazil. Outwardly, the slaves worshiped the Catholic saints, but secretly, they prayed to their own African gods and goddesses.

Macumba celebration in Rio de Janeiro.

Other forms of African-Brazilian spiritualism are practiced outside Bahia. In Rio de Janeiro, there is *macumba*, developed about 200 years ago; and in São Paulo, there is *umbanda* ("oom-BAHN-dah"), a mixture of *candomblé*, *macumba* ("mah-COOM-bah") and the spiritualism of a 19th century French mystic named Allan Kardec. None of these religions should be confused with voodoo or the Cuban practice of *santería* ("sahn-teh-REE-ah"), in which bad luck can be directed at one's enemies.

Candomblé has a pantheon of gods and goddesses, each with his or her own characteristics and traditional costumes and colors. The gods, called *orixas* ("orh-re-SHAHS"), are representative of the forces of nature, but they also have human aspects. Xango, for instance, is the god of thunder and lightning, and he is said to be proud and stubborn. Oxalá is the creator god who in his youth was said to be a brave warrior; in his older form, he is the tranquil god of birth. Oxum is associated with water, and she is said to be vain and beautiful. Yemanjá, the goddess of the sea, is peaceful and stately.

Up until 20 years ago, most followers of *candomblé* still kept their true faith somewhat hidden. Now that blacks in Brazil have begun to make themselves heard, their religion has come out of the closet, so to speak. Today, people of all colors have turned to *candomblé* for guidance and direction.

During the *candomblé* ceremonies, worshipers dressed in the clothing of gods and goddesses become possessed by the spirits. As the drums beat loudly and rhythmically, their bodies shake, their eyes roll back in their heads, and they enter a deep trance in which each person takes on the personality of his or

her chosen god or goddess through specific dance steps. The possession rituals, as well as other temple rites, are presided over by powerful priestesses. People come to the *candomblé* temples to ask for help with their personal and even medical problems. The religion offers them a kind of spiritual psychotherapy in a safe, communal atmosphere.

Jews and Protestants Most Brazilians are either Catholic or followers of African-Brazilian religions, or a combination of the two. But there are also some 150,000 Jews in Brazil, many of whom fled to South America to escape persecution in Germany. In Brazil, they are free to practice their own religion.

In recent years also, Catholicism and *candomblé* (and its offshoots) have lost millions of followers to fundamentalist Christian sects. These churches preach the power of the individual—in conjunction with Jesus Christ—as the catalyst for change. A woman may join them in an effort to find the patience to deal with a disobedient child or a husband who drinks or beats her.

The poor especially have turned to evangelical churches in an effort to find the spiritual strength to confront and perhaps overcome the wretchedness of their lives.

Bahian cuisine

The Bahian cook was immortalized in Jorge Amado's *Dona Flor and Her Two Husbands*, in which the heroine uses her culinary talents to keep her husband happy, and his *Gabriela, Clove and Cinnamon*, in which one of Gabriela's many attributes is her skill in the kitchen.

Bahian cuisine has its roots in the food of West Africa, the region that furnished Brazil with most of its black slaves, but it also has elements of Indian and European cooking. Through their food, Bahian women express their African heritage and continue their cultural traditions.

A standard ingredient of both cuisines is *dendê* ("deh-DAY") oil, made from the palm tree. *Dendê* oil is dark red in color and has a distinct, powerful aroma when heated. It is often mixed with thick, sweet, fresh coconut milk and used to cook classic Bahian seafood and chicken dishes. One especially well-loved Bahian dish is called Shrimp Caruru. It consists of freshly caught local shrimp sautéed in butter, onion, parsley, and green pepper, and combined with okra (a common ingredient in Bahian dishes of African origin), coconut milk, dried shrimp, manioc flour and *dendê* oil.

Native Brazilians

When the first Portuguese colonists came to Brazil in the early 16th century, the country was inhabited by millions of native Indians. Today, fewer than 200,000 Indians belonging to about 175 different tribes are left. Some of the Indians live semi-traditional lives on reservations set aside by the government while others live in undesignated regions throughout the interior. A quarter of the Indians live in the Amazon territories.

Threats faced by the Indians Even today, previously unknown tribes are still being found in remote parts of the country. One of the largest remaining Indian tribes, the Yanomami, have recently been displaced by tens of thousands of opportunists who have swarmed to northern Brazil in search of gold.

Other people of Indian heritage living in the vast rain forests of the Amazon have had their existence threatened by cattle ranchers who wish to raze rubber trees to make grazing land for cattle. Since the late 1960s, the rights of Brazil's Indians have been protected by a government agency.

A Yanomami Indian woman in a cotton hammock.

Immigrants

Brazil experienced several waves of immigration in the late 19th and early 20th centuries.

Italians came in large groups from the 1880s through the 1920s. Some worked as agricultural laborers in the coffee fields of southern Brazil to replace slaves that had earned their freedom. After several years of working the land and saving money, many Italians moved to cities and began successful small businesses.

Immigrants from Portugal, Spain, Germany, the Mideast, and Eastern Europe also came to Brazil in significant numbers during this period. The Germans in particular were excellent farmers, and even today the southern part of Brazil is dotted with thriving German farming communities. Portuguese nationals continue to emigrate to Brazil today, as do people from various Latin American nations.

Japanese-Brazilians After 1908, the Japanese began emigrating to Brazil in large numbers. Today, as surprising as it sounds, Brazil has the largest Japanese population (1.2 million) outside Japan. When they came to Brazil in the early 20th century, the Japanese intended to stay only until they had accumulated substantial savings. Instead, they stayed on and invested their money in land, which they used to grow fruits and vegetables. Today Japanese-Brazilians

A Japanese woman in São Paulo. Although many of the Japanese originally came to take jobs as unskilled laborers, they are now among the wealthiest, most respected people in Brazil.

Lifestyle Among the tribes, gender roles have remained somewhat the same over the generations. Women are still primarily responsible for planting and gathering food and going through the long process of making manioc flour. They bring the water to the village, watch over the children and keep the huts clean. The men continue to fish and hunt for wild game, as well as clear the fields for the first planting. They also oversee the tribe's spiritual life, and women often take a backseat in important rituals and ceremonies.

grow much of the produce for the populous state of São Paulo. They also own large businesses and banks. There are important Japanese politicians, judges, and college professors.

The Japanese have managed to assimilate into Brazilian society, yet they have retained their cultural identity. They celebrate Japanese holidays, eat Japanese food at home and adhere to Japanese values like punctuality, efficiency, and a strict work ethic. The older generations tend to be conservative about male and female roles within the family, but the younger generations are more liberal in their attitudes.

In São Paulo, where most Japanese-Brazilians live, there are Japanese neighborhoods with Japanese schools, shops, and restaurants, as well as several Japanese newspapers. While the first immigrants never mastered the Portuguese language, many of their children and grandchildren know little of the Japanese language. Some can speak it, but do not know how to read and write the difficult characters. In the past few years, tens of thousands of Japanese-Brazilians have taken crash courses in their native language so they can return to Japan and take advantage of the country's economic boom. In Brazil, they can earn only the equivalent of $200 dollars a month, while in Japan, where they are employed in menial jobs that Japanese nationals refuse to take, they can earn about ten times that figure.

The great internal migration

Only about 50 years ago, Brazil was a rural agricultural society. Today the country is overwhelmingly urban. In fact, nearly 75% of all Brazilians live in large cities. Twenty percent of these either live in Rio de Janeiro, which has 11.4 million people, or São Paulo, which has just over 18 million.

A Japanese-Brazilian girl. A high percentage of Japanese-Brazilians are college graduates.

Poor children in Acre, in the Amazon.

behind poverty, disease, and malnourishment, not to mention a poor education system and a life of hard labor with little hope of advancement. The infant mortality rate was also high.

Some rural dwellers, especially young women, migrated by themselves; others came with their entire families. Most, however, had friends or relatives from their hometowns in whose urban neighborhoods they eventually settled. Few had jobs or leads to jobs when they migrated, and so they ended up trading one form of deprivation for another. Men had more difficulty finding employment; women, at least, could turn to jobs in domestic service.

Many migrants who came to Rio de Janeiro and São Paulo ended up settling in one of the many *favelas* that exist among the upscale high-rise buildings. Today Rio de Janeiro has approximately 450 different slum neighborhoods, many on steep hillsides. One out of three *cariocas* lives in one. *Favela* life is dirty and dangerous, due to the lack of proper water and sanitation systems and the gangs of drug dealers that live there.

Migration to the cities During Brazil's economic boom in the 1960s and 1970s, millions of rural Brazilians, especially inhabitants of the drought-ridden northeast, flooded the cities in search of a more prosperous way of life. They left

The poor northeast The rural northeast comprises nine Brazilian states and about 20% of the country's land. Northeasterners live in a region filled with misery and hopelessness. In fact, the northeastern region has been called the most impoverished area in the entire Western Hemisphere.

Life in a *favela*

In 1960, *Child of the Dark*, the diary of a female *favela* dweller called Carolina Maria de Jesus, was published and met with critical acclaim. The simple eloquence she uses to describe her difficult life in the "garbage dump," as she calls it, is unforgettable. Much of what she says is applicable to life in a *favela* today.

Carolina, a black woman, lived in a shack in a São Paulo shanty town with her three children. She had no official job, but she managed to eke out a living by collecting paper and other junk from the trash cans of the rich and selling it to a junk dealer. Sometimes she had almost nothing with which to feed her family and had to resort to using bones she had found in the garbage to make soup. "How horrible it is to see your children eat and then ask, 'Is there more?' This word 'more' bounces inside a mother's head as she searches the cooking pot knowing there isn't any more," she wrote in her diary.

Despite her wretched existence, Carolina was proud of her children, her black skin, and her independence. Although she had only two years of schooling as a child in Minas Gerais, she learned to read and write quickly and, as an adult, turned to writing to escape from her troubles. Her book is an astonishingly honest portrait of the daily trials of a black woman who only wants to escape hunger and leave the *favela*. After the book was published (it was discovered by a journalist who met Carolina while covering the opening of a park in the *favela*), she loaded up her possessions and moved to a suburb where she could send her children to decent schools and live without hunger and fear.

chapter five

Profiles of Women

The six Brazilian women who are profiled in this chapter include a princess, a pioneer for women's rights, a record-breaking aviator, a flamboyant singer, a critically acclaimed fiction writer, and the country's most beloved entertainer. They are all outstanding in their own fields, thus functioning as heroines and role models for other Brazilian women. For their achievements, they deserve a place in the history of Brazilian women.

Princess Isabel

Princess Isabel de Bragança, the daughter of Brazil's second and last emperor, is considered a heroine by many Brazilian women today.

Although Isabel accomplished much during her reign in the last years of the monarchy in the late 19th century, she is famous for an historical act of overwhelming importance to Brazilian society: in 1888, she signed the proclamation that ended slavery in Brazil and gave 700,000 blacks their freedom. For this, Isabel has been called "The Redeemer." Her heroic act has been reenacted by African-Brazilian members of Rio de Janeiro's best samba schools during the Carnival parade.

Isabel's father was the benevolent Emperor Dom Pedro II, the son of the noble Empress Leopoldina. Pedro was only five years old when his father, an inadequate leader, abdicated the throne in his favor. At the age of 14, Dom Pedro II became the ruler of Brazil, a position he maintained with grace and dignity for nearly 50 years.

Opposite and right:
Princess Isabel. The picture opposite shows her in her wedding gown.

Princess Isabel signing the Emancipation Proclamation that ended slavery in Brazil.

clamation, thereby offering absolute freedom to Brazil's 700,000 slaves. The document freed the slaves unconditionally—without requiring them to buy their liberty from their owners.

Although this act made Isabel a heroine to Brazil's slaves and many of its early feminists, it endeared neither the princess nor her family to the white plantation owners who were now compelled to pay wages to their labor force. In addition, Isabel had lost some favor with her subjects upon her marriage to an arrogant and domineering French nobleman, Gaston d'Orléans, Comte d'Eu, who refused to integrate himself into Brazilian society and never learned Portuguese.

On November 15, 1889, the democratic Brazilian army led a revolt against the monarchy, forcing Dom Pedro II and his family to flee their homeland and seek refuge in Europe. The Brazilian Republic was born and Isabel never returned. She died in 1921 at the age of 75.

Dom Pedro II saw to it that his daughter Isabel, born in 1846, was well-educated and well versed in his own progressive philosophy. When he was compelled to return to Europe several times in the 1870s and 1880s, he trusted Isabel to run the country. For those years, Isabel was the only woman to occupy a position of political power in the entire country. In the event of Dom Pedro's death, Isabel was to succeed him to the throne.

Emancipation for slaves On May 13, 1888, in her father's absence, Isabel signed Brazil's Emancipation Pro-

Isabel's signing of the Emancipation Act "is an excellent testimony to the energy and capacity of woman."
—*Brazilian feminist publication, 1889*

Bertha Lutz

Bertha Lutz, more than any other Brazilian woman of her day, was responsible for bringing the issue of women's suffrage to the forefront in the 1920s and 1930s and guiding it through its successful passage. An intelligent, worldly woman of the upper-class, Lutz was the true mother of the Brazilian feminist movement.

Bertha Lutz was born in São Paulo in 1894. Her parents sent her to Europe for schooling, where she completed a degree in science at the University of Paris in 1918. When she returned to Brazil, she attended law school in Rio de Janeiro and successfully obtained a second degree. Heavily influenced by the progress women had made in Europe and America, Lutz was convinced that Brazilian women too could make strides toward equality.

Bertha Lutz *(left)*. She helped bring about suffrage for Brazilian women.

> "Work is the most powerful instrument in the hand of a woman....I consider that in Brazil, the true 'leaders' of feminism, correctly understood, are the innumerable young women who work in industry, in commerce, in teaching, and in other spheres of human activity."
>
> —*Bertha Lutz, women's rights pioneer*

Pioneering the women's movement In 1918, she voiced her views in a letter that appeared in a Rio de Janeiro newspaper. She said, "We must educate women so that they can be intellectually equal and be self-disciplined. We must educate men so that they become aware that women are not toys created for their amusement, and so that, when observing their wives and sisters or remembering their mothers, they understand and are completely convinced of the dignity of women."

Lutz founded the League for Female Intellectual Emancipation in 1920. In 1922, she was personally responsible for the admittance of women to Rio de Janeiro's finest prep school, the Colégio Dom Pedro Il. She achieved this by going directly to the education minister whom she knew in connection with her own prestigious job at the National Museum.

Lutz represented Brazil at the first Pan-American Conference of Women held in Baltimore in 1922. Upon her return, Lutz remodeled the League into what became a powerful national organization called the Brazilian Federation for the Advancement of Women (or the FBPF).

Although many members of the FBPF were, like Lutz, from the upper classes, some represented the middle class—the part of society that Lutz was most interested in helping. The FBPF was concerned with changing the legal status of women, obtaining the vote, and instituting fair labor laws and educational policies for women.

Lutz and her followers decided not to confront the public with demands concerning such volatile issues as sex education and divorce, undoubtedly a wise decision in a country that simply was not ready for drastic changes in its social system.

Suffrage for Brazilian women By the 1930s, the FBPF had constituents from every Brazilian state and was the most impressive women's group in the nation. It counted both doctors and home-makers among its members and was cohesive in its ideology. It strived to obtain the vote without upsetting Brazil's social order. Members of the group believed that women could fight for their rights without giving up their duties as mothers and wives and without losing their femininity.

In 1932, when Brazilian women obtained the right to vote, Lutz was personally responsible for its passage. Sensing that the political climate was right, Lutz and other highly placed members of the FBPF went straight to President Getúlio Vargas with their demands—and came away with his acquiescence.

Rights of working women After the passage of women's suffrage, Lutz worked on what she considered an important goal: the economic emancipation of women. She was disturbed by the treatment of lower-class women in the workplace and by the fact that, after work, they still faced hours of domestic responsibilities at home. Lutz also worked to increase job opportunities for rural women, institute laws concerning maternity leave and help improve the lives of lower-class children and domestic servants.

Lutz's political career Lutz was instrumental in writing the section on women for the 1934 constitution. In 1936, she became a member of the Chamber of Deputies, where she spoke out strongly for the establishment of a special governmental body to deal solely with women's issues. Before this proposal could be taken up, however, the congress was closed in 1937 by Getúlio Vargas, and did not reopen until 1945.

Although Lutz's political career at home was halted, she continued to

represent Brazil internationally in the decades that followed. Even as late as 1975, at the age of 81, Lutz traveled to Mexico City to attend the International Women's Year conference. She died in 1976.

Bertha Lutz devoted herself to women's causes for nearly 60 years.

Anésia Pinheiro Machado

In 1922, when 19-year-old Anésia Pinheiro Machado earned her pilot's license, few Brazilian women even drove cars, much less flew airplanes.

Anésia Pinheiro Machado, a well-decorated female pilot.

successes, and she was encouraged by friends and family alike. In 1922, she said that even as a child, she had wanted to surmount "restrictions inherent to [her] conditions as a woman." She later joined the most prominent Brazilian women's organization, Bertha Lutz's FBPF, and gave speeches on career opportunities for women.

After obtaining her license, Pinheiro Machado did more than just fly for pleasure. She made solo flights, earned an international license and earned money making short trips for paying passengers.

Her aerial feats In June 1922, she won international acclaim when she broke a Brazilian record by flying to an altitude of nearly 14,000 feet. At that height, she said she became so cold in her open-cockpit plane, that a passenger had to rub her hands to keep them from freezing.

That same year, she learned how to do aerial stunts and made a remarkable flight from São Paulo to Rio de Janeiro, the first such flight executed by a woman. Although today this nonstop interstate flight takes less than an hour, in 1922 it took four times that long and required four stops for refueling. The devices used today for navigation did not exist then, and Pinheiro Machado had to use landmarks such as mountains and railroad tracks to keep the plane on course.

A flying start Pinheiro Machado first became interested in flying as a young girl when an aviator made a stop in her hometown. Being an adventurous type, she decided that flying was something she could enjoy, despite her young age and the fact that the field was dominated by men.

Newspapers in São Paulo covered her first flight as well as her subsequent

When she landed to refuel, she said in a 1987 interview for *Américas* magazine, "It was a real event. The local people were wildly enthusiastic. Many had never seen an airplane, much less one with a woman pilot."

Career and marriage After her important inter-state flight, Pinheiro Machada became a journalist for a Brazilian newspaper and wrote articles on aviation. She later married a pilot, and they made many flights together. In the 1940s, she qualified as a private and commercial pilot and an instructor.

Later she worked periodically in the government as a kind of flying diplomat. Once she made an historic intercontinental flight from New York to Rio de Janeiro, stopping in Argentina, Paraguay, and Uruguay to encourage goodwill between Brazil and those countries.

Decorations Pinheiro Machado has been decorated more than 50 times for her aerial exploits. She won the Amelia Earhart Medal and became the first woman to win the impressive Aviation Eagles Award. She has also received honorary licenses from the French, Italian, and Chinese governments.

In 1987, she remarked that she was amazed at the "spectacular progress" made in flying since 1922, but she felt that women—in aviation and elsewhere—still had far to go in the movement toward equality.

Carmen Miranda

In 1939, Brazilian singer Carmen Miranda left Rio de Janeiro for the United States and introduced samba music to the world. To Americans growing up in the 1940s and 50s, she was the symbol of Latin America—its freedom, its spontaneity, and its musical creativity.

Carmen Miranda at the London Palladium—her first London appearance.

Carmen Miranda is famous for her headgear and platform shoes. Here, she tops her glitzy costume with a miniature lighthouse.

Her outlandish clothes and ostentatious fruit-laden headdresses were admired by millions of fans. For a while she was the highest paid woman in the United States.

Born for the stage Maria do Carmo Miranda da Chunha was born in 1909 near Lisbon in Portugal. The following year, she and her family migrated to Rio de Janeiro. While in her teens, Miranda began singing live on the radio.

She later made several popular records and appeared in five Brazilian movies. Once she moved to Broadway, where she did stage shows, and Hollywood, where she made 19 movies, she achieved international success. Many of her American-made movies were simple musical revues for the screen, written to show off her excellent voice and her colorful, imaginative choice of dress and headgear. For example, in *Doll Face*, made in 1946, she wore a glowing lighthouse on her head. In other productions, she wore Bahian-style turbans sprouting tropical fruit such as coconuts, mangoes, pineapples, and bananas.

Mixed reception To Brazilians living in the 40s and 50s, Carmen Miranda— probably the world's best-known Brazilian woman in her day—was a source of both national pride and embarrassment. Although Carmen Miranda had had some success in the recording and movie industries in Rio de Janeiro, she was not considered the best representative of the rich world of contemporary Brazilian music. Her music was seen as dated and her costumes vulgar.

Today many Brazilian musicians have come to terms with their ambiguous feelings about Miranda and see her as an artist who simply was not appreciated by Brazilians during her lifetime.

Her legacy A collection of her music has been rereleased on compact disc in Brazil and her former critics have found themselves surprised by her musical dexterity and sense of humor. Fashion designers have begun to copy the clothes she wore (most of which she designed), and some singers have started to echo her style.

Tourists and Brazilian fans can visit an entire museum devoted to Carmen Miranda near Flamengo Beach in Rio de Janeiro. There, her glittery gowns, eight-inch heels, and amazing hats (never made with real fruit) are on display, as well as the many awards she received until her death from a heart attack in 1955. The music played at high volume over the museum's stereo system is, of course, pure Carmen Miranda-style samba.

Clarice Lispector

Clarice Lispector has been called the preeminent Latin American female prose writer of the 20th century. Because she was a woman and wrote in Portuguese, she was all but unheard of outside Brazil until recently.

Born in the Ukraine in 1925, Lispector and her family moved to the northeastern city of Recife when she was still a baby. As a teenager, Lispector settled in Rio de Janeiro, where she completed a law degree.

At 19, she published her first novel, *Near to the Wild Heart*, which met with immediate critical acclaim from several established literary critics.

After her marriage to a diplomat, she worked periodically as a journalist while continuing to write fiction. She had two children and lived in Europe and the United States for a length of time. In 1959, she was divorced from her husband and soon thereafter returned to her native Brazil.

Clarice Lispector. Her novels provide insightful studies of women's lives.

> "I have never had what can be truly defined as an intellectual life. Even when writing, I use my intuition rather than my intelligence. One writes as one loves. No one knows why they love just as they do not know why they write."
>
> —*Clarice Lispector*

Before her death in 1977, she had completed nine novels, several collections of short stories, important translations of English works, books of essays and several stories for children.

Writing about women's lives

Lispector's short stories have been compared to those of the American writer, Flannery O'Connor, and her novels to those of the French existentialist Jean-Paul Sartre.

Feminist critics have called her the "new prophet of the female world" because of her insightful, often painfully real studies of women's lives. She has influenced many of Brazil's contemporary female writers who have patterned their all-knowing narrators after Lispector's.

Her writing habits

Lispector's writing habits were unusual. She carried a pad with her at all times and took notes on interesting conversations she overheard and ideas that suddenly came to her. From these notes, she would write her final piece; she never changed her original words, although sometimes she added or deleted material. Often, she would write in the middle of the night while listening to music.

Hour of the Star

This was Lispector's last and, some critics say, finest novel. Published in 1977, it chronicles a short time in the life of a young woman named Macabéa, an uneducated, innocent orphan who comes to the sprawling, overcrowded city of São Paulo from a small town in the impoverished northeast. She finds lodging in a ramshackle building where she must share a room with three other women. Macabéa is a classic outsider; she is ignorant of the urban way of life and has little idea of how to survive in it. She is poor, unattractive, and dirty. She fails miserably in her job as a typist. In a pitiful way, she attempts to imitate the dress and manners of Gloria, the glamorous office girl with whom she works, and she dreams of becoming a movie star. Seen against the huge, dirty mass that is São Paulo, Macabéa looks so small and insignificant that our hearts break for her.

Eventually, Macabéa meets a man, Olimpico, in a city park, and in her innocence, thinks he may be a potential boyfriend. Olimpico, however, detests Macabéa for her ugliness and lack of sophistication, and ends up seducing Gloria, her officemate. When Macabéa learns of the betrayal, she seeks the help of a fortune teller, who tells her that she will soon meet a rich man driving a Mercedes who will make her happy. In ecstacy, Macabéa walks onto the street and is hit and killed by just such a man in a fancy car. Her death, like her life, goes unnoticed.

In *Hour of the Star*, which was made into an award-winning feature film by Brazilian director Suzana Amaral in 1985, Lispector gives us insight into the life of a poor, simple-minded girl thrust into the faceless sprawl of the Brazilian city. Lispector's book is so rich and so real, and her character's life so tragic, that it can be seen as a vivid, timeless portrait of Brazilian womanhood.

Xuxa

A blond, blue-eyed Brazilian woman named Maria da Graça Meneghel, or Xuxa ("SHOO-shah") as she is known, is the most popular entertainer in Latin America. In 1990, *Forbes* magazine listed her among their 40 highest paid entertainers; with an income of $19 million that year alone, she came in 37th, between writer Tom Clancy and actor Mel Gibson. Her four and three-quarter hour television show airs every morning on Brazil's biggest network, the Globo station. It is watched by an estimated five to 10 million viewers. Needless to say, it is the highest rated show in Brazil, except for a very important soccer match. Some 60 products, with sales of $52 million in l991, bear her name. There are Xuxa dolls, Xuxa rubber sandals, Xuxa skateboards, even Xuxa soup. To Brazilians, she has been likened to Barbie, only she is more perfect in her looks; to Madonna, only she is more popular; and to the Ninja Turtles, only she is more marketable. Xuxa is a Brazilian empire.

Xuxa, at the age of 29, was voted one of the world's most beautiful people by *People* magazine in 1992.

Young fans Who is Xuxa's audience and why do they adore her so? Xuxa's biggest fans are children.

It is difficult to get tickets for her television show. When she goes on a national tour, she sells out stadiums and arenas (even when the cheapest seats cost $12), and thousands of children go home disappointed.

After a concert, she is mobbed by little ones screaming her name and begging her to sign their homemade Xuxa photo albums. Xuxa travels with several bodyguards at all times to discourage overexcited fans. In 1991, three would-be kidnappers were actually shot and killed before they could get their hands on her.

Stage attire During the morning "Xuxa show"—which is part variety, part games and contests, many children dressed like Xuxa appear on stage with her. They wear miniskirts, high boots, and short jackets with glittery touches. Their hair is done Xuxa-style in bobbing high ponytails. Behind Xuxa stand her backup singers and dancers: six or seven young girls who also have blond hair and blue eyes and are similarly attired.

Xuxa's background Xuxa is a heroine to many Brazilians because she is a self-made woman. Her grandparents were of Austrian and Italian heritage, and she was brought up in a middle-class military family. Her first break came when she signed a modeling contract with the Ford agency. Her face became more recognizable to the Brazilian public when she dated the country's most famous man, the soccer star Pelé.

Her first television show, which was produced by the Globo station's competitor, was not a great success. After she made her first album, however, she signed with the Globo station, and her popularity soared.

Achievements So far, she has made four records (which have sold 15 million copies) and several movies. She has her own comic book, which sells more than 200,000 copies a month. Xuxa's total net worth is estimated at over $100 million. Her television show is now broadcast in other Latin American countries as well as on an American cable channel. She has plans to start a show in English to expand her market.

Her influence and values To many parents, Xuxa is a role model for their children. She is talented and self-driven, a positive force in a society that is beset with severe social problems.

Despite Xuxa's appearance of sexuality, she is quite conservative in the values she preaches on stage. She warns children repeatedly to keep away from alcohol, drugs and cigarettes. She reminds little ones to brush their teeth regularly and look before crossing the street. She is an animal lover and an

Within the image: **F**íjate bien   **C**uida tu sonrisa

environmentalist and supports several charitable organizations.

To some parents, she is an outrage. Her appearance, they say, is promiscuous; it invites children to look and act beyond their years. Her blondness, so unrepresentative of Brazil's mostly dark-skinned population, offends many people because it sets a standard of beauty that is unattainable.

The Xuxa obsession Some parents criticize Xuxa for encouraging children to want what they cannot have, whether it be a ticket to her concert or the newest Xuxa-endorsed toy.

Xuxa herself appears to be a bit baffled as to why she is so popular, although she certainly revels in the attention children pay her.

Xuxa promoting toothpaste. Product endorsements bring her the most revenue.

"There is a child born every day in Brazil babbling my name. There are children who haven't learned to say 'Mommy' or 'Daddy,' but they say 'Xuxa.' It's something that makes me very happy."
—*Xuxa, in a 1991 interview in the Washington Post*

Sonia Braga

Sonia Braga is probably the best-known Brazilian actress in her native land and in North America. She has played the female lead in several Brazilian films based on classic stories.

She was Gabriela in the movie based on Jorge Amado's novel, *Gabriela, Clove and Cinnamon*, and Dona Flor in his *Dona Flor and Her Two Husbands*. She landed the lead in many critically acclaimed films made in the United States, such as *Kiss of the Spider Woman*, *Moon Over Parador*, and also, *The Milagro Beanfield War*, which was directed by Robert Redford.

Braga's background

Sonia Braga was born in Maringá, a town in the south of Brazil, to an upper-middle-class family of mixed race. Her father was half black and half Portuguese and her mother was of Portuguese and Indian extraction.

In 1958, when she was eight years old, her father suddenly died, leaving her mother to raise seven children alone. At the age of 14, Braga was forced to stop going to school so she could take a job as a typist. A friend Braga knew mentioned her to a filmmaker, and she got a part in a children's television show. When she was 17, she was hired to act in a Brazilian soap opera, an important step in a country where soaps, or *novelas* as they are known, are regularly watched by an enormous percentage of the population.

First film role

Two years later, Braga was cast in her first film, *Dona Flor and Her Two Husbands*. She played the role of Dona Flor, a beautiful and loyal married woman with a charming but philandering husband who dies of a heart attack during a raucous Carnival dance in the movie's first scene. When Dona remarries a gentlemanly pharmacist who is kind to her but a bit on the boring side, her dead husband's ghost appears—but only she can see him. Throughout the course of the movie, Dona cannot decide whether she wants to banish the ghost or to keep him around to add spice to her marriage.

Braga excelled at this complicated role and developed a screen personality that is both sultry and uninhibited, and angelic and innocent at the same time.

Her famous role as Gabriela

Braga went on to star in the Brazilian films, *I Love You* and *The Lady on the Bus*, and achieved greater international fame with the American-produced *Gabriela*, the story of an impoverished, filthy woman picked up in an old slave market in Bahia by a man looking for help in his restaurant. Once she washes herself, though, she is transformed into a beautiful woman.

The man falls in love with her, despite the differences in their social classes. Soon, he begins to try to civilize Gabriela; he buys her shoes and clothes and even marries her in an attempt to

make her all his own, but ultimately she prefers to be shoeless and independent, and even ends up transforming him.

More recent roles In 1991, she starred in a movie made for the Lifetime cable channel called *The Last Prostitute*. In November of that year, she began filming *The Flying Camel* with actor and director Roy Scheider. In it, she plays a beautiful Italian woman who meets two unusual men in Tel Aviv, Israel.

Views Braga is extremely proud of the strong female roles she has played and hopes that her films will encourage Brazilian women to stand up for themselves.

She is also modest about her own beauty and accomplishments and sees her break into acting as the lucky fate of a skinny, ugly teenager who just happened to meet the right person at the right time. She now lives in the United States.

Sonia Braga. For all her work abroad and sophisticated Hollywood veneer, Braga says that she considers herself to be a Brazilian through and through.

Benedita da Silva, Brazil's first black congresswoman.

Benedita da Silva

What Benedita da Silva has achieved in a male-dominated society like Brazil's, where blacks make up almost 45% of the population but have the least power and economic stability, is nothing short of amazing. In 1986, as a member of the left-wing Workers' Party, Benedita da Silva, or "Bené," as she is called by her constituents, became the nation's first black congresswoman. (Today the Chamber of Deputies still has fewer than 10 black members and only about 25 female members)

Friend of the less fortunate In 1992, at the age of 50, she became the spokesperson for Brazil's "less fortunate."

Her primary concerns are fair treatment for blacks, women, domestic laborers and urban street children, as well as vital educational and environmental issues. She is not afraid to challenge Brazil's oldest institutions, such as the police force and the judicial system, and has had modest success in her endeavors.

Growing up in a favela Da Silva is passionate about defending the rights of the downtrodden because she was once one of them. She was born in a *favela* in Rio de Janeiro to a family of 13 children.

Like her grandmother, who was a slave, da Silva began working at a very young age. At five, she delivered laundry for the washerwomen in her *favela* and begged for food scraps at outdoor markets. By the time she was 11, she had a factory job. She was often teased because she wore the same dress every day or because of her kinky hair.

In school, she was told that she couldn't possibly be as smart as the white children in her class and that, because of her color and her poverty, she would not amount to anything. Later, she worked as a maid, a cook, and a street vendor.

Sometimes, she lived on the streets with her husband, a biscuit seller, and their children. "The whole time I was growing up," da Silva says, "I was made to feel that blacks were inferior to whites. Today not much has changed. Blacks still suffer from racism."

Da Silva did manage to excel at school, despite the doubts of her teachers, and eventually scored high marks in a civil servants' examination. Although her test results led to a job as a nurse's assistant, she still was not satisfied with what life in Brazil had to offer her and black *favelados* (*favela* dwellers) like her.

> "I never desired to be a politician for its own sake. I just wanted to be a woman, a black woman, a *favelada*, who didn't end up inanimate like so many others. I wanted to do something to improve this community."
> —*Benedita da Silva*

Entering politics She joined the Workers' Party, and in 1982 was elected to the city council of Rio de Janeiro. From there, she was elected to her present position in the Chamber of Deputies with the help of her second husband, who has devoted himself to her political career.

Some say that from that position, she will run in and win the mayoral election in Rio de Janeiro.

Benedita da Silva, a role model for other *favelada*s.

"I am the exception to every established rule in this country. In reality, there's no opportunity for people like me."
—*Benedita da Silva*

An eloquent speaker Da Silva is known for her remarkable oratorical abilities. Her speeches are dramatic and persuasive. She speaks from the heart. Perhaps some of her dynamism can be traced to the passionate sermons she hears regularly at her church, an evangelical congregation called the Assemblies of God.

Her faith and her roots Although she was raised with both Catholic and African religions, she had little personal faith or hope for her people until she joined the Protestant sect, which has helped direct the lives of countless black *favelados*. "My faith has led me to comprehend that God created all things for all people," she said. "So how can I accept so much inequality?"

She spends much of her time in the Brazilian capital of Brasília, but still maintains a home in Rio de Janeiro, in the *favela* where she was born, so as to keep in close contact with the city's poor. The kids in her neighborhood all know which house is hers and how far she has come.

Benedita fights for the rights of the less fortunate in Brazilian society.

chapter six

A Lifetime

T hroughout the history of Brazil—except for the last two decades—sex roles have been sharply defined. Girls were brought up to be passive creatures of the home, while boys were encouraged to make their way in the outside world. According to the dictates of Catholicism, women were to preserve their virginity at all cost until their marriage. Men, however, were expected to indulge in sexual exploits from an early age. Women were the nurturers, while men were the providers.

With the rapid urbanization of the last few decades, sex roles have become less delineated for many Brazilians. Women are demanding equality with men in the workplace as well as the home. For those living in traditional, rural areas, however, sex roles have remained almost the same as in the past. In this chapter, we will explore the traditional models for women and men, and discuss what it is like to be a woman in Brazil throughout all of life's major phases: childhood, adolescence, marriage, motherhood, and old age.

Whether in rural areas (*opposite*) or in cities (*right*), women have traditionally been defined by their maternal roles. But through education and employment, they are breaking out of the traditional mold.

Traditional sex roles

Ask a woman to characterize male society in Brazil and she will start with a single, powerful word: macho (or *machão*, in Portuguese). But what does macho really mean and what is its female counterpart? Are Brazilian men truly macho, or is that a stereotype that is wrongfully applied to all Latin American men?

The younger generation, especially those with some education, are not locked as firmly into their gender roles.

What is macho behavior? By definition, machismo refers to an exaggerated sense of male pride or power. The macho man exudes self-confidence. He is strong, virile, and dominant. He handles himself with ease in the outside world.

He considers women to be of two types: the demure, virginal, and domestic sort to marry, and the indecent, impure type to keep as a mistress. The macho man practices a double standard: he is concerned with family honor and decency, so he marries a compliant woman of a high class, but to exercise his own masculinity and maintain his freedom, he sleeps with other women who are often of a lower class.

Marianismo The feminine counterpart to machismo in Latin America is called *marianismo* (the root word of *marianismo* is "Mary," referring to the Virgin Mary). Women who subscribe to *marianismo* are saintly, generous, nurturing, and infinitely patient with, and forgiving of, their macho husbands. Although they suffer from their husband's philandering, they enjoy the power they exert in the domestic sphere and are aware of their own moral superiority.

Do these codes really exist? Whether or not machismo and *marianismo* truly exist in Brazil today depends on the social class and economic standing of the family in question.

People living outside Brazil's urban

areas, those from the far northeast, the interior states, and the far south, for instance, tend to be more conservative, and sex roles tend to be more traditional. In the cities, however, the rules do not always apply. In some families, the fathers, mothers, and grandparents are of the old school, but their children and grandchildren are not locked as firmly into their gender roles. Women are free to follow the careers of their choice (although some women still shy away from the strictly masculine professions like engineering), and virginity is not necessarily a requirement before marriage.

In very poor urban households, with single mothers and absent fathers, the model does not apply. But in typical families comprised of both parents and several children, these codes most likely contain an element of truth.

Machismo is probably less rampant than it was 10 or 20 years ago. But Brazilian society, to be sure, is more macho than American society.

Housewives waiting to fill their buckets with water from a stream. The macho code that insists a woman's place is at home exists in some families.

From the time a little girl is old enough to speak, her family teaches her to be feminine. She is dressed in frilly or lacy clothes, in particularly feminine colors like pink and white.

A macho man's views There is even a Brazilian Macho Movement made up of men who want to keep women at home and leave the important decision-making to men. One of the movement's founders, Luiz Carlos Jacare Ladeira, thinks that women have lost their femininity in recent years by taking jobs that belong to men and by not playing their traditional, passive roles. Ladeira said, during a convention of machos in Rio de Janeiro in fall 1991, that in response to women's cries of dis-

crimination, the government had revoked laws banning women from being truckers, construction workers or miners. But he retorted, "Who wants to go home to a wife who smells of cement and has big muscles?" Ladeira believes that women should stay at home. The very few Brazilian women at the convention did not agree.

Birth and the girl child

During the early colonial period, when the family fortune was passed through the daughter at the time of her marriage via the dowry system, parents often preferred girls to boys. With daughters, parents were able to choose their child's future spouse and retain a measure of control over the family's financial future. Toward the end of the colonial era, the dowry practice was phased out. The economic changes in society had given men opportunities to make their fortunes other than through inheritance or marriage, and men and their families then had the upper hand in selecting spouses.

Today, there is a decided preference in Brazilian families for boys, at least among more conventional families. If a woman has a female child first, or a succession of female children, her friends and family might console her and tell her that she shouldn't worry, that she can try for a boy next time.

Different upbringing Girls are taught to be demure and gentle in their actions, to be caring of others, and to be mommy's little helper around the house. They are not to be overly demanding or to question authority. Boys, on the other hand, are encouraged to be rambunctious and to speak their minds. They are not expected to do domestic chores and are allowed to run wild more than their sisters. Boys are often very attached to their mothers, who give them an enormous amount of attention, but they are ridiculed by their older brothers and

Baptism rite

All Brazilian children, no matter what their social class, are baptized according to the Catholic tradition to welcome them into the Christian faith. Although Brazilians do not necessarily demonstrate their Catholicism on a daily basis, especially those who practice African-Brazilian religions as well as Catholicism, all consider baptism an important initiation rite.

Babies are usually baptized when they are about a week old. Often there is a small ceremony at the church, to which close friends and family members are invited, and a larger party afterward at the house of the host. Food is served, and the women usually go into the bedroom to see the baby and share tips on mothering while the men gather in groups and talk.

The parents of the newborn often choose a godmother and godfather for the baby to ensure that somebody will look after the child in the event of the parents' deaths. In some families, the connections made between children and godparents last for many years. The godparents might give the child birthday gifts every year, and when the child grows up, they might help him or her find a job.

other male family members if they show the least signs of having feminine characteristics.

Boy or girl, most parents show great affection for their children in public and in private. Children of middle and upper-class families are pampered by both their parents and their nannies, or *babás*, as they are known.

Brazil's street children, left to fend for themselves by their poor working mothers, turn to a life of hustling, begging, and crime.

for themselves in the cities. Unfortunately, when they get there, they find that they have few skills that can translate into a well-paying job. The men find it most difficult to find jobs, so the women are forced to work. Usually, the only choices open to them are housekeeping or childcare. Only the lucky ones find jobs in factories or stores.

An unemployed husband A husband's unemployment puts a great deal of stress on the family. Sometimes he decides to leave his wife and children; other times he turns to drinking for consolation, and domestic violence erupts. It is rare, however, for him to simply stay at home and take care of the children.

The children's plight While the women are at work (and many of them live with their employers during the week), the children are often left by themselves. Many do not go to school, and most have no food to eat. Therefore, they turn to the streets to beg or steal food with other gangs of children. Many children take up glue-sniffing or other cheap drugs and spend as much time as they can getting high or mugging people for the money to get high.

In Rio de Janeiro, groups of very daring boys and girls make a game out of riding on top of commuter trains that go as fast as 60 miles per hour. In 1988, about 200 children (called *surfistas* or surfers) were killed, and 500 were

Brazil's street children

In Brazil, the disparity between the rich and the poor is enormous. What is different about the Brazilian social system compared to that in the United States is that, in Brazil, the terrible economic conditions of the last decade have led to the weakening of the middle class. Families are often either very wealthy or very poor. Few are in the middle class.

Difficulty finding jobs As jobs continue to disappear in agricultural areas, people dream of making a better life

injured when they fell from the trains or got caught in the electric cables hanging above the trains. After spending all day in the streets, some children go home to sleep at night, but others simply find a dry place on the street for sleeping.

A large-scale phenomenon Today Brazil's urban street children number in the millions, although nobody knows exactly how many there are. Estimates range from 3 to 15 million. In large cities in the United States, most people have become familiar with the sight of a homeless adult sleeping in a cardboard box, but very few can imagine what it would be like to live among an entire society of neglected children. (For a realistic, but very disturbing view of life as a street child, see Hector Babenco's film *Pixote*, shot in Brazil using real street children as actors.)

In the past, most street children were boys, but today there are many female street children, some of whom turn to prostitution (even at a very young age) to make a living. Most of the children living on the streets are the offspring of single, black mothers.

All of Brazil's street kids live in constant fear of being caught by the authorities, who either send them to reform schools or orphanages, where they are rarely adopted. Many of the girls who are adopted are simply taken in by families who use them as unsalaried maids.

Out of a total population of 140 million people, 45 million are children living in abject poverty, 15 million children do not get enough to eat every day, 12 million children are abandoned by their parents, 8 million children live on the streets, 7 million children are handicapped, and between 4,000 and 5,000 children are murdered each year.

Crime and violence According to Brazilian law, children under the age of 18 cannot be prosecuted for their crimes. Policemen get to know the repeat offenders and even beat and torture them in an effort to prevent them from committing another crime. In the past four years, thousands of street children have been murdered—by other children who run with drug gangs and by the police themselves, much to the horror of most Brazilians.

Helping the children The nation has not turned its back on the children. In Rio de Janeiro alone, there are some 600 organizations to help street children. Most children have been approached and offered a meal or temporary shelter.

The National Children's Crusade helps kids stay in school and find jobs. The National Movement of Street Boys and Girls of Brazil, established by the children themselves, helps fight for children's civil rights.

> **"The Brazilian people need to be reminded that there is a basic right that comes before any other: the right to live. If we don't secure this right, nothing else matters."**
> —*Tânia Maria Salles Moreira*
> *public prosecutor and children's rights advocate*

In São Paulo, members of the military police play with children every week as part of a program to help encourage relationships between the police and them. Other street kids attend a circus school on weekends where performers teach them circus tricks and help bolster their confidence.

Since 1990, Tânia Maria Salles Moreira, a female public prosecutor living in Rio de Janeiro, has been fighting to convict the people responsible for killing street children. The murderers are either cops or hit men hired by neighborhood drug lords who do not want the children impinging on their territory. She has had some success, despite the many death threats she has received and the fact that many of her witnesses get killed before they can testify.

Adolescence

In colonial days, once a young girl reached adolescence and began to look more womanly, her parents shielded her from contact with men for fear that she would be seduced and thus lose her virginity. By the ages of 13 or 14, she would be safely married and would begin starting a family, preferably a large one.

Today of course, these social rules have been relaxed. Only in the most traditional families are adolescent girls separated from boys. In most cases, girls and boys go to school together, even when attending private Catholic schools. They socialize at school and elsewhere when they reach high school age. Both girls and boys are encouraged to work hard in school although the average family is likely to channel a girl's interests toward feminine pursuits.

Dating Teenagers do not usually "date" in the old-fashioned sense. They are more likely to go out in groups of boys and girls. Sometimes they meet at the beach or the mall; other times they all go to the movies. Rarely does a boy pick up a girl at her home and come in to meet her parents. If he does, the parents will think of the friendship as something serious.

In the past, girls did not flirt with boys, as men were always supposed to be the aggressors. Today teenage girls often flirt with boys, but usually in public places, as a group activity.

Controlled by parents Although parents allow their daughters some freedom, they expect them to come home at a

stipulated time and to follow their rules, even if these rules are thought of as unreasonable.

In general, Brazilian parents exercise more control over their teenagers than many American parents. Brazilian parents tend to keep close tabs on their children's behavior by asking a lot of questions about where they are going and what they will be doing.

Even when a girl has begun working, she is expected to live at home until she marries. This may be partially due to economic constraints because few single people can afford apartments of their own.

The "coming out" party In well-to-do families, girls celebrate their 15th birthdays in an elaborate way that outdoes most American "sweet 16" parties.

Brazilian parents generally keep a tight rein on their daughters.

A woman's appearance

All over the world, Brazil is synonymous with sex appeal, with the mulatto woman atop the carnival float wearing nothing but a few strategically placed sequins, and the girl on the beach in her "dental floss" string bikini. Of course, not all women in Brazil wear so little, but they do tend to be less inhibited about their bodies than women from North America.

Through their dress, Brazilian women draw attention to their sexuality. They enjoy being looked at and admired by men and want very much to look feminine. (This does not necessarily mean that women dress to lure men into their beds; a woman wants to be admired but she also wants the right to say no.) Their necklines are usually lower than those of North American women, their pants tighter, and their skirts shorter. Jewelry and makeup are used liberally, and hands and feet are well taken care of. Women may age, but they do not want to look older, so they dye their hair and try to keep their bodies in good shape. As one Brazilian woman in her 30s said, "Growing old in Brazil is feared, and we fight against it."

Most Brazilian women take great care with their appearance, whether they are going to the grocery store, the office, or out to dinner. They feel strongly that certain types of clothes are only appropriate for certain settings; a tight bathing suit or shorts, for instance, belong on a beach and not in a shopping center. A fashionable suit belongs in an office, and jeans (pressed and unfaded, never frayed) belong only in the most casual settings. Brazilian women prefer natural fabrics like cotton and silk to hot and cheap-looking synthetics. They constantly update their wardrobes and keep up with what's going on in the European fashion centers.

Originally, the 15th birthday party was meant to be a version of the "coming out" or debutante ball. It allowed the girl to dress up like a grown-up for the first time and to meet men who might be interested in marrying her.

Today the 15th birthday party has none of those connotations. It is simply an expensive birthday party with its own set of rituals. Often, the debutante will choose 14 other girls and their dates to be her attendants. All the girls will wear frilly, feminine gowns that match (although the birthday girl's might be slightly fancier), and the boys will wear matching suits.

The girl sometimes carries a candle that her father lights, and it then is passed from girl to girl. The party includes traditional ballroom as well as contemporary dancing and is held at a social club or rented hall. Dinner and drinks are served.

Education and careers

In Brazil today, there are many children who do not go to school, and even those who do often drop out before completing

College students
with their teacher
in São Paulo.

their studies. Among most families, however, there is a strong commitment to education for their children. Both girls and boys are expected to excel in the classroom and to put in the necessary hours after school for homework.

At the college level, there are currently more female students enrolled than male students. Many female college students study hard in order to enter the professions.

In 1970, for instance, there were approximately 19,000 women professionals in Brazil, including engineers, architects, dentists, economists, professors, lawyers, and doctors. By 1980, there were about 95,800 women in these fields.

Despite the inroads made into the professions, most Brazilian women who are employed work in typically female occupations.

Working outside the home is an economic necessity for many Brazilian women.

Types of work Out of a total female working population of 18 million, about 25% work in domestic service, 13% in agriculture, 13% in factories, 13% in sales, 10% in elementary education, 16% in lower-level office jobs, and about 6% in seamstress jobs. Women are also concentrated in nursing and social work.

Compensation Despite the fact that women now make up more than 37% of the work force, they are paid considerably less than men for the same work. On average, women are paid about 50% less than men, and gross salary inequities have been found in teaching, farming, and other professions. Although Brazilian law forbids discrimination based on sex, most female employees, especially those in the lower-level jobs (such as farming and domestic service), are not registered with the government, and minimum wage laws are therefore not able to be enforced. When registered with Brazil's National Social Security Institute, women are entitled to benefits such as maternity leave, unemployment and

Working women and job stress

According to a 1991 survey conducted by *Claudia*, Brazil's most popular women's magazine, and published in the March 1991 issue of the American magazine, *McCall's*, Brazilian working women experience less on-the-job stress than women working in the United States, Australia, Germany, and Japan. Fewer Brazilian women thought about work once they came home compared to women from the other countries, and fewer felt unable to control the work pace while on the job. More Brazilians were victims of "verbal abuse in the office," however, and most felt that they were both underpaid for their efforts and unlikely to be promoted in the future. According to Célia Pardi, *Claudia*'s editor-in-chief, "Low pay causes stress, but friendships and freedom gained from working compensate." Approximately 70% of the respondents, in fact, stated that the most important reason for working was the feeling of independence they gained.

When Brazilian women did feel stress on the job, they often relieved it after working hours by taking a long weekend, exercising, dancing, relaxing, doing yoga, or getting extra sleep. Of all the nationalities surveyed, they were the least likely to take a day off, but the most likely to consult a doctor or psychologist if things got really rough. Within the office, however, Brazilians (like Americans) usually decided to "do nothing and endure" rather than take the problem to the boss.

disability insurance, pension plans, and medical care.

Problems of working wives Many husbands have accepted the fact that their wives must work, but if they themselves are unemployed, seeing their wives as providers can upset their sense of male pride, resulting in stress within the family. Finding suitable child care is a problem that is faced by many families, especially those who have neither a parent nor a full-time maid to act as babysitter. Brazil has its share of day-care centers, but, as in many countries, well-run, affordable ones are in short supply.

For many working mothers, the toughest time of the day is after work, when they come home tired, but are faced with a slew of domestic chores for which they, as women, are responsible. This phenomenon of working both on the job and at home, called the "double day," is common in Latin America, where husbands are reluctant to help with household chores. If a woman is able to afford domestic help, this problem is minimized, but it still exists because the woman of the house is ultimately responsible for directing the activities of the maid. If the maid is sick, for instance, the woman must take over the chores. If a child is sick, the mother is the one to miss work, sometimes even if the father is not employed.

Brazilian women today have more freedom in choosing their life partner.

society was completely tied to that of her husband. If he was an honored member of the community, then she too was respected. Women were dependent on their husbands for everything. Men were expected to protect and provide for the family at all times.

Marrying later In Brazil today, women marry much later in life than they did in colonial times. The average age for marriage is currently 22.6 years for women and 25.9 years for men. Women often spend several years working before they marry. During this time, they usually live at home and contribute some of their salaries to the family budget.

Engagement In Brazil, engagements usually last longer than they do in the United States. If the engagement period is hurried or lasts less than a year, people tend to think that the couple is getting married because the woman is pregnant.

Many men still prefer that the women they marry are virgins or have not had extensive sexual experiences with other men. In some lower-class communities, loss of virginity is not considered shameful, but pregnancy out of wedlock is.

Although men used to follow the custom of asking the bride's parents for her hand in marriage, this is rarely done in Brazil today. Women receive a single ring when they are engaged, which they

Marriage

In the past, marriage was the highest accomplishment of a Brazilian woman. Only through marriage (or by becoming a nun) could a girl hope to leave her father's home. A woman's status in

wear on the right hand. During the wedding ceremony, they remove it from the right hand and place it on the ring finger of their left hand.

Pre-nuptial rituals Before a wedding, the bride-to-be's friends give her a small wedding shower, often held in the home of her closest friend. During the shower, the bride's friends tease her and sometimes play tricks on her. She also receives gifts, usually something modest and practical, such as kitchen items.

The groom's friends throw him a bachelor party. These "saying goodbye" parties, as they are known, are usually held in bars or clubs, and the groom often receives small bar-related gifts from his friends.

The marriage ceremony The wedding ceremony in Brazil is usually very important to the bride. She and her family may spend years planning and saving money for it, and they may spend more money on that one day than they would spend in ten years.

Many parents pay for their daughter's weddings, but some couples take on the burden themselves. Brides have been known to spend so much on their wedding dress that they must pay the dress company in installments for years after the wedding day. A grand wedding is a symbol of status in Brazil, just as it is elsewhere around the world.

There are two types of marriage ceremonies in Brazil: the civil and the religious. Some people marry simply in front of a judge and invite only their closest friends and relatives. Others marry at the courtroom during the day and in the church at night. Still others combine the two in an elaborate church service, which includes a mass (sometimes videotaped) followed by a large party in the bride's home or at a country club or rented hall. Traditional wedding food includes the cake, champagne, pastries, candies, and chocolates. Generally, a band is present, and there is music and dancing.

A mixed marriage.

> "When the father leaves the house the household trembles; when the mother leaves it, the house crumbles."
> —*an old Brazilian saying*

Motherhood

Although Brazilian women tend to have fewer children than they used to, motherhood is something that most women want to experience.

Starting a family early Immediately after the wedding, the newlyweds will start getting pressure from their relatives to have children. Many couples now wait two or three years before starting a family in order to save money, but others begin to try right away.

The maternal role Once a woman has given birth to her children, she assumes a great responsibility for their development. The mother takes nearly complete charge of the raising of the children, although she may defer to her husband in matters of great importance. It is she who pushes the children to excel and who can take some credit for their scholastic achievements. It is she who gives them a moral education, thereby molding them into decent human beings.

Sometimes, a woman's maternal instincts are so strong that she lavishes her attention and affection not only on her own children but also on the children of her relatives, such as neices and nephews, and the children of her friends and colleagues as well. Perhaps this is not peculiar to Brazilian mothers—the strong maternal figure can be found in any other culture.

Caesarean births

Although in rural areas, babies are still delivered at home by midwives, most babies born in Brazil's cities are delivered by well-trained doctors in relatively modern hospitals.

While in the United States and much of Europe it is now common for pregnant women to first attempt to give birth the natural way (vaginally, with few drugs) and have a Caesarean section only as a last resort, in Brazil many women prefer to give birth by Caesarean section. Overall, about 33% of all babies are born by Caesarean section in Brazil. In publicly funded and private hospitals however, the rates soar to 66% and 80% respectively.

Following the doctor's schedule One reason why Caesarean births are so common is that hospitals in Brazil do not often have the staff required to wait out a natural birth. A Caesarean birth is faster and can be scheduled by the doctor, who often does the operation

before the mother's due date. Once the delivery becomes predictable, the doctor is no longer at the mercy of nature's own timing and can perform many operations in one day, and thereby collect more fees.

Also, the government-sponsored health insurance does not pay for painkillers or anesthesia given to mothers in pain during natural labor. With a Caesarean section, the entire operation is paid for, and mothers never experience labor pains.

Feminists in Brazil have long been disturbed by the high rate of Caesarean births because they feel that women should give birth naturally, not according to a doctor's schedule.

There are also risks accompanying a Caesarean operation. Babies born by Caesarean section have a greater chance of catching respiratory illnesses, and mothers who undergo unnecessary operations are at risk of developing complications because of infection or improper administration of anesthesia.

Motherhood has always given Brazilian women a sense of power within the family.

Just a few decades ago, it was normal for mothers to have 10 or 12 children, but now families, especially urban ones, choose to have only two or three children.

thirds of married women in the childbearing years use birth control, especially the pill, although the Catholic Church approves of only natural methods of contraception.

Employers' discrimination Since 1988 when the Brazilian government approved a four-month maternity leave, many employers have been reluctant to hire women in the childbearing years for fear that they will be required to pay them during maternity leave. Some employers simply refuse to hire young women unless they can produce a medical certificate proving that they have been sterilized. Other employers will pay for a woman's maternity leave, but will only allow her to resume her job after seeing the sterilization form. Many Brazilian women, especially the feminists who helped draft the new maternity laws, have been appalled at this treatment but realize that little can be done about it.

Family planning

Just a short time ago, Brazil was considered a nation with a booming, almost out-of-control population. Today the nation's birthrate is comparatively low for women in both urban and rural areas. In 1970, the birth rate was 5.75 children per mother, but today it is only 3.2. Experts attribute the decrease in family size to the nation's poor economy and widespread adoption of family planning techniques. More than two-

Abortion

Abortion, which is not legal in Brazil except in the case of rape or if the woman's life is in danger, is nonetheless widely practiced. In the United States, where abortion is legal, some 1.6 million abortions are performed every year. In Brazil, the figure is somewhere between 1.4 and 2.4 million. As might be expected, hundreds of thousands of women are victims of botched abortions every year, and hundreds of them die. Some abortions are performed in proper clinics, but others take place in unprofessional surroundings using dangerous methods. Occasionally, the police raid the clinics and make arrests, but mostly they turn a blind eye to their existence.

Many Brazilians believe that abortion should be legalized, but few politicians are eager to back the issue for fear of alienating members of the Catholic Church. Women's rights activists in particular, who have long been in favor of legalization, have staged many pro-choice rallies. At the very least, they hope for well-run government-sponsored family planning clinics and sex education programs in schools.

Divorce

Divorce was legalized in Brazil in 1977. According to the law, a couple must be legally separated for three years before a divorce will be granted. If a woman is abandoned by her husband, she can get a divorce after five years. Men can remarry immediately after the divorce papers are signed, but women must delay their remarriage for 270 days. Women are almost always granted custody of the children, and fathers are required to pay child support. Only one divorce per person is allowed in Brazil.

Despite the fact that divorce is now legal in Brazil, it is still considered a social stigma. Separation, whether formal

Sterilization, formally known as tubal ligation, is the second most common form of birth control in Brazil. Nearly 30% of married women in Brazil have undergone sterilization—an astonishingly high rate compared to the United States (17%), Peru (8%), and even China (24%). Many poor women choose to have their tubes tied to avoid future pregnancies and keep their families small. The operation is usually performed just after the birth of a baby by Caesarean section so that the doctor's fees are kept at a minimum.

or informal, is deemed socially acceptable in many communities, but divorce is still thought of as a sin. As one Brazilian woman said, "After a divorce, life is over for a woman, especially if she has children."

Divorced women are often blamed for the failure of the marriage, and are therefore feared by single men. A divorced woman is often ashamed of her status and will refuse to discuss her divorce. Divorced men, on the other hand, have little trouble dating and remarrying.

Among poor communities in Brazil, a significant percentage of women are abandoned by their husbands or partners and thrust into the position of breadwinner. These women are usually black and, because of discrimination, have little chance of finding a good job.

The honor defense

Up until quite recently, it was common for a man to inflict violence on and even murder his wife if she was even suspected of adultery and walk away without legal consequences. In many cases, even if the man was brought to trial, he could plead what is called the "honor defense"—the moral right of a man to harm his wife if she damaged his honor by having an affair—and the jury would let him go free. In 1980 and 1981, in the state of São Paulo alone, some 700 men used the honor defense as a justifiable reason for killing their wives. In the northeast and the interior, "honor" killing is even more prevalent. Brazilian feminist Rose Marie Muraro said in a 1991 *New York Times* article, "In the interior of the country, it is easier and cheaper for a man to hire a gunslinger to kill his wife than to get a divorce and to separate the property."

In 1991, the Brazilian high court of appeals ruled that the honor defense could not be applied to cases in which wives were murdered by their jealous husbands. The court said that "self-esteem, vanity, and the pride of the Lord who see his wife as property" were responsible for bringing men to murder their wives, not the defense of honor. Despite the landmark ruling, individual juries have continued to allow such men to go free, proving the point that social rather than legal norms are still the most influential in Brazil.

Adultery

One factor of Brazilian life that puts severe stress on a marriage, and which can often lead to divorce, is adultery. In Brazil, it is quite common for married men to have extramarital affairs. From a very young age, a boy is encouraged to display his masculinity, especially through his sexual exploits.

In his early teens, an adolescent boy is often brought to a prostitute by his father or brothers for his sexual initiation. He will spend increasingly more time with groups of men who discuss sex freely and attempt to outdo each other with sexual jokes and anecdotes. Sex, to a man, is a healthy activity with little guilt or shame attached. Even after marriage, a man is encouraged to exercise his masculinity through sexual activities.

Attitudes to extra-marital affairs Traditionally, Brazilian women were expected to accept their husband's adultery as another burden of married life. They were not supposed to ask pointed questions about his affairs or to demand that he cease to engage in them. Today, however, things appear to be changing. In many middle-class communities, adultery is looked down upon by both women and men. Women are having affairs now as well—in many cases, the consequences of having an affair are disastrous.

To many Brazilian men, nothing is more damaging to the male ego than becoming a "cuckold," that is, the partner of an adulterous wife. It is considered acceptable and even normal for a man to flirt with women, even married women. On the other hand, a woman who flirts or leaves her husband for another man can be the victim of serious domestic violence.

Domestic violence In the last ten years, Brazilian women's groups have been responsible for bringing domestic violence against women to public attention. In the 1980s, many women conducted anti-violence marches in Brazil's cities as part of what was called the "Lovers Don't Kill" campaign. They also worked to establish anti-violence organizations, including the all-female police precincts that now exist throughout Brazil.

Old age and death

Traditionally, older women are treated with great respect, especially by their grown sons.

Old parents are traditionally taken care of by their children

It is common for women—and men—to cry openly when a close friend or family member dies.

The matriarch Even in the past, older women were in many cases exempt from the laws of gender that applied to younger women. They were permitted to speak their minds, to make major decisions, even in business, and to direct the lives of their adult children.

The culture of the matriarch still exists in Brazil, at least in some families. Adult children often set up house near their parents and visit them several times a week. Many Brazilians would never consider moving across the country away from their parents, although this is a common occurrence in the United States.

Filial piety If a parent dies, the child will take the other parent in without hesitation as it is considered his or her duty. The elderly in Brazil rarely live in

Other Brazilian rituals and rites of passage

- In Japanese-Brazilian families, funerals are attended by hundreds of guests. One week after the funeral, the same group meets in the home of the deceased to pray at the family altar and share a meal. During the first 49 days after death, the spirit of the dead is supposed to reside in the home, and people are free to visit and pay their respects to it. After the 49th day, the spirit is free to go to heaven.
- Every June 13th, unmarried men and women pay their respects to their patron saint, St. Anthony. Single women offer him prayers and money so he will find them a husband. In rural areas, large outdoor barbecue parties are held and fake wedding ceremonies are enacted.
- The Nambiquara tribe of Mato Grosso state celebrates the onset of puberty by confining a girl to a special hut. After a certain period of time, she is released to the accompaniment of dancing and music, and thereafter is considered a woman by all members of the tribe.
- Upon reaching old age in the Mundurucú tribe of the Amazon, women are given equal status with the dominant males and allowed to behave as their peers. An older woman is allowed to sit wherever she likes (instead of in the back of the hut), eat with the men (instead of after them) and be forthright in her opinions.
- In the African-Brazilian religions, women play the primary roles in initiation rites. Priestesses direct the ceremonies and are imbued with special powers that allow them to be possessed by the gods.

private nursing homes. For some, they are too expensive, but for most, they are scorned examples of familial neglect.

The funeral When an elderly person dies in Brazil, the funeral usually takes place soon afterward—within 24 hours if possible. Embalming is rarely done. The *velório* ("veh-LAW-ray-oo") or death watch is held the night before the funeral in the home of the deceased or at a funeral parlor. Close friends and family usually visit the bereaved during the *velório* and spend time praying with and talking to the family.

The funeral itself is attended by family and friends, but after the burial service, only members of the immediate family will go back to the house of the bereaved. Unlike in the United States, it is not a Brazilian custom for a buffet to be served to guests after a funeral. Widows do not dress in black for a year after the death of their husbands as was the case in the past, but conservative, religious women are usually seen in dark colors during this period. Catholic masses for the deceased are held seven days, 30 days, and one year after the funeral.

Women Firsts

Mirtes de Campos	In the late 19th century, she became the first Brazilian woman to attend law school in Rio de Janeiro, the first woman to be accepted into the Brazilian bar, and the first woman to litigate in a Brazilian court of law.
Maria Augusta Generosa Estrela	(b. 1861) She traveled to New York in 1875 at the age of 14 to attend medical school. In 1882, she returned to Brazil as the nation's first female doctor.
Maria Luiza Fontenele	In 1985, she became the first female mayor of Fortaleza, the capital of Ceara state.
Gardenia Goncalves	In 1985, she became the first female mayor of São Luiz, the capital of Maranhao state.
Princess Isabel	(1846–1921) Known as "The Redeemer" to many Brazilians, she signed the proclamation that ended slavery in Brazil in 1888 and gave 700,000 blacks their freedom. She was the first woman in Brazil to carry out a political act of such historical importance.
Carolina Maria de Jesus	Upon the publication of her diary, *Child of the Dark*, in 1960, she became the first *favela* or slum dweller to write a bestseller.
Maria Quiteira de Jesus	During the struggle for Brazilian independence, she dressed herself in men's clothing and joined the troops fighting against the Portuguese. In 1823, she became the first Brazilian woman to be decorated by an emperor for her efforts in battle.
Rita Lobato Velho Lopes	In 1887, she successfully completed a degree in a Bahian medical school, becoming the first woman to earn a Brazilian medical diploma.
Bertha Lutz	(1894–1976) As Brazil's foremost feminist, she was the first woman to effectively lead the campaign for women's suffrage. She was also the founder of the Brazilian Federation for the Advancement of Women.
Anésia Pinheiro Machado	(b. 1903) She is a famous aviator who earned international acclaim by being the first Brazilian (of any sex) to fly at an altitude of 14,000 feet, the first to make an intercontinental flight, and the first woman to fly from São Paulo to Rio de Janeiro.
Anita Malfati	(1889–1964) She was an important avant-garde artist of the 1920s who was personally responsible for setting the Brazilian modernist movement in motion.
Zélia Cardoso de Mello	In 1990, she became first female cabinet member in the history of Brazil. Her tenure as Minister of the Economy came to an end in 1991, however, after it was discovered that she was having an affair with the married Minister of Justice.
Carmen Miranda	(1909—1955) A singer and a dancer, she was the first Brazilian woman to popularize the art of samba to an international audience. At the height of her popularity in the 1930s and 1940s, she was one of the wealthiest female entertainers in the world.
Carlota Pereira de Queiroz	This important Brazilian feminist became the first female member of Congress in 1933 and the first female associate of the National Academy of Medicine.
Francisca Roiz	In 1603, Roiz became the first person—male or female—in all of São Paulo to obtain a commercial license. She opened a small food store.
Benedita da Silva	As Brazil's first black congresswoman, she is considered by many to be the voice of the nation's less fortunate. Her primary concerns are fair treatment for blacks, women, domestic laborers, and urban street children, as well as vital educational and environmental issues.
Luiza Erundina de Souza	In 1989, she became the first female mayor of São Paulo, South America's largest city.

Glossary

babá ("bah-BAH") A Brazilian nanny.

baiana ("BUY-yahn-ah") Woman from the northern state of Bahia.

bandeirante ("bahn-day-RANT-ee") A male raider who made expeditions into the Brazilian interior during the colonial era to bring back Indians to be sold into slavery.

candomblé ("cahn-dom-BLEH") An African-Brazilian religion that involves spirit possession and other mystical rites and rituals.

carioca ("car-ree-AW-ca") A resident of Rio de Janeiro.

delegacia ("dell-e-gah-SEE-ya") A women's police station.

dendê ("deh-DAY") A cooking oil, extracted from the palm tree, used in African-Brazilian dishes.

emancipation The act of setting free from bondage or disability of any kind.

enfranchisement Extending the right to vote to certain sections of the community.

favela ("fa-VELL-ah") An urban slum or shantytown.

initiation rite A ceremony by which a person is initiated into a fraternity, club, etc.

Luso-Brazilian Portuguese-Brazilian.

machismo An exaggerated sense of male pride or power.

manioc Any of several tropical American plants, shrubs, and trees of the spurge family having fleshy, starchy roots.

mucama ("moo-CAH-ma") A black female house slave during colonial times.

macumba ("mah-COOM-bah") A form of African-Brazilian spiritualism practiced mostly in Rio de Janeiro.

musical revues A type of musical show consisting of loosely connected skits, songs, and dances.

mulatta A woman of mixed race; also a symbol of the Brazilian female erotic ideal.

novela ("no-VELL-ah") A Brazilian soap opera.

orixás ("orh-re-SHAHS") The gods, in the religion of *candomblé*.

patriarchal society A society where the father or the eldest male is recognized as the head of the family or tribe, descent and kinship being traced through the male line.

paulista ("POW-lee-stahs") A resident of São Paulo.

psychotherapy Treatment of mental disorder by any of various means involving communication between a trained person and the patient and including counseling, psychoanalysis, etc.

scurvy A disease characterized by weakness, anemia, spongy gums, bleeding from the mucous membranes, etc.

samba A style of music and dance brought to Brazil from Africa.

santería ("sahn-teh-REE-ah") A type of African-Cuban spiritualism that has been likened to voodoo.

senzala ("say-ZELL-ah") Portuguese word for slave quarters.

suffrage The right to vote.

typhus An acute infectious disease transmitted to people by the bite of fleas, lice, etc, and characterized by high fever, headache, and an eruption of red spots on the skin.

umbanda ("oom-BAHN-dah") A form of African-Brazilian spiritualism practiced mostly in São Paulo.

urbanization A change from country to city life.

velório ("veh-LAW-ray-oo") The "death watch" held for the deceased before a funeral.

Further Reading

Alvarez, Sonia E.: *Engendering Democracy in Brazil: Women's Movements in Transition Politics*, Princeton University Press, Princeton, New Jersey, 1990.

Brant, Alice, trans. Elizabeth Bishop: *The Diary of "Helena Morley,"* The Ecco Press, New York, NY, 1977.

Freyre, Gilberto: *The Masters and the Slaves*. Alfred A. Knopf, New York, NY, 1971.

Guillermoprieto, Alma: *Samba*, Alfred A. Knopf, New York, NY, 1990.

Hahner, June E.: *Emancipating the Female Sex: The Struggle for Women's Rights in Brazil, 1850–1940*, Duke University Press, Durham, NC, and London, 1990.

Harrison, Phyllis A.: *Behaving Brazilian: A Comparison of Brazilian and North American Social Behavior*, Newbury House Publishers, New York, NY, 1983.

de Jesus, Carolina Maria, trans. David St. Clair: *Child of the Dark*, E.P. Dutton & Co., Inc., New York, NY, 1962.

Miller, Francesca: *Latin American Women and the Search for Social Justice*, University Press of New England, Hanover, NH, and London, 1991.

Murphy, Yolanda and Robert F. Murphy: *Women of the Forest*, second edition, Columbia University Press, New York, NY, 1985.

Nazzari, Muriel: *Disappearance of the Dowry*, Stanford University Press, Stanford, CA, 1991.

Parker, Richard G.: *Bodies, Pleasures, and Passions: Sexual Culture in Contemporary Brazil*, Beacon Press Books, Boston, MA, 1991.

Patai, Daphne: *Brazilian Women Speak*. Rutgers University Press, New Brunswick, NJ, 1988.

Sadlier, Darlene J., editor: *One Hundred Years after Tomorrow: Brazilian Women's Fiction in the 20th Century*, Indiana University Press, Bloomington, IN., 1992.

Stein, Stanley J.: *Vassouras, A Brazilian Coffee County, 1850-1900*, Harvard University Press, Cambridge, MA, 1957.

(Note: Many of these Brazilian films are available in the foreign film sections of large video rental stores.)

Bye Bye Brazil (1980): The story of Brazilian modernization as seen through the eyes of a band of traveling performers; directed by Carlos Diegues.

Gaijín, Roads to Freedom (1980): The story of the early Japanese-Brazilian experience; directed by Tizuka Yamasaki.

Hour of the Star (1985): The film adaptation of the novel by Clarice Lispector about an unsophisticated young girl who migrates to São Paulo; directed by Suzana Amaral.

How Nice to See You Alive (1989): A documentary about eight women imprisoned and tortured under the Brazilian military dictatorship; directed by Lucia Murat.

Pixote (1981): The story of a Brazilian street boy; directed by Hector Babenco.

Xica (1982): The story of Xica da Silva, an exceptional black slave woman in the 18th century; directed by Carlos Diegues.

Index

Picture Credits

Abril Imagens: 25, 40, 49, 50, 59, 62, 63,
    81, 86, 95, 96, 98, 99, 115.
Agência Estado: 83, 85, 89.
Apa: 41, 71, 112.
Bernard Sonneville: 5 (bottom), 28, 45,
    51, 66, 68, 114.
Brazilian embassy: 24, 56, 82.
Hulton-Deutsch Collection Ltd: 87.
John Maier: 6, 7, 8, 9, 10, 11, 27, 31, 35,
    36, 38, 42, 48, 53, 54, 58, 60, 65, 67,
    72, 73, 74, 76, 76, 77, 78, 79, 91, 93,
    101, 102, 103, 104, 109, 111, 118,
    121, 122.
Life: 3, 21, 37, 106, 117.
Maier Media: 39, 57.
The Image Bank: 5 (top), 34.
UPI/Bettmann: 46, 80, 88.
Victor Englebert: 12, 75, 100.

*The author wishes to thank Doretta Fuhs,
Alice Kina Pearl, Sirley Wagner, Jill DuBois,
and A. Headenphye for their help and
patience in the creation of this project.*